Contents

About the authors

Anna Dixon is Deputy Director of Policy at the King's Fund. She has conducted research and published widely on health care funding and policy. She has given lectures on a range of topics, including UK health system reform and patient choice. She was previously a lecturer in European Health Policy at the London School of Economics and was awarded the Commonwealth Fund Harkness Fellowship in Health Care Policy in 2005–6. Anna has also worked in the Strategy Unit at the Department of Health, where she focused on a range of issues including choice, global health and public health.

Arturo Alvarez-Rosete is a Researcher, Health Policy at the King's Fund. He specialises in public policy and public administration, with particular interest in the structures of government and governance and the policy process in the NHS. He is currently working on developing best practice models for health policy making and on international comparisons of health regulatory systems. His recent publications include a chapter on citizen's attitudes towards the NHS for the 2005 British Social Attitudes survey and a *BMJ* article on the effects of devolution and diverging policy across the NHS. Arturo holds a PhD in Politics from the University of Nottingham and has been a visiting lecturer at several universities in Europe and Latin America.

Acknowledgements

The authors wish to thank Nicholas Mays and Rudolf Klein for invaluable comments on earlier drafts. The final report also benefitted from discussions with colleagues at the King's Fund who helped to refine the ideas contained within this paper.

Summary

The report provides a critical discussion of proposals for an independent NHS board put forward by political parties, health professional bodies and stakeholders. These proposals are primarily concerned with giving the NHS operational independence. Advocates of the idea claim that an independent board would reduce both micromanagement by the Department of Health and central political interference in the day-to-day running of the NHS. In the report we argue that an independent board would be limited in its ability to achieve these aims, and examine how these issues were dealt with in the past; in particular, how the balance was struck between central control and local autonomy, and the extent to which it was possible to separate out policy from operational management of the NHS. We suggest that these issues have been difficult to resolve historically and we question whether an independent board could do so more effectively. We argue that the raft of current health system reforms begins to give greater operational independence to some health care organisations and reduces the ability of ministers to interfere in the management of the NHS; this could be taken further. We suggest a number of alternative options to an independent board that we believe could address some of the perceived and real problems of the current system of governing the NHS. These would help secure a better balance between public accountability and local autonomy within a more devolved health care system.

Introduction

The question of whether the NHS in England should be given greater independence from politicians has been widely debated over the past year. At the heart of these debates is the proposal to create an independent board. This is not a new idea (Hutton 2000; NHS Alliance 2000; Conservative Party 2003). Indeed the King's Fund itself proposed the creation of an NHS corporation at arm's length from government (King's Fund 2002; Dewar 2003).

Amid the financial crisis, in spring 2006, the issue was revived in the *British Medical Journal* (Godlee 2006). The idea put forward was for an 'independent NHS authority' which 'would be run by a board of governors responsible for managing health care within a set budget and a broad political framework' (Godlee 2006). During autumn 2006, each of the main political parties entered the debate.

The models of 'independence' that were being proposed were not always clear, and various analogies were drawn. The former Health Minister, now Chief Secretary to the Treasury, Andy Burnham (2006), proposed that the NHS should have a constitution similar to the BBC Charter, which would be renewed every 10 years. Suggestions were made that the former Chancellor and current Prime Minister, Gordon Brown, was planning to hand over the NHS to an independent board in the same way that he had given the Bank of England an independent role in relation to monetary policy. It seems that his interest in the idea was somewhat overstated. The Labour government has since retreated from the idea (Blair 2007). Patricia Hewitt (2007) made her scepticism clear in one of her final speeches as Secretary of State for Health:

> *If the NHS was a country, it would be the 33rd biggest economy in the world, larger than new European Union transition economies like Romania and Bulgaria. Would the Prime Minister of such a nation*

*seriously propose today to take the entire economy and put it under
a single independent board, every organisation in the hands of one
owner, run as one entity?*

The Conservative Party has, however, continued to pursue the idea.
It proposes to 'establish an autonomous NHS Board to oversee the
commissioning of NHS services' (Conservative Party 2007, p 16).
More recently the Liberal Democrats have suggested creating a
commissioning and advisory authority. They assess that this option
would be the 'most open and accountable framework', although the
main thrust of their policy is still directed at achieving local democratic
accountability (Lamb 2007). A number of the different models for an
independent board have been reviewed elsewhere (see British Medical
Association 2007; Glasby *et al* 2006; NHS Confederation 2007).
Edwards (2007a) describes in some detail seven models for changes in
the governance of the NHS and highlights the differences in the extent
of independence that an executive agency, executive non-departmental
public body or public corporation would have from government.

Proponents of an independent board believe that it would shield the
NHS from political interference in the day-to-day running of the NHS,
although it is not always clear precisely what this means. Generally,
politicisation is used to mean excessive ministerial interference in the
implementation of policy and operational matters, rather than the
involvement of politicians in developing health policy as such. Closely
associated with this is the charge that the current arrangements create
an over-centralised NHS. By this they usually mean that the Department
of Health is too involved in micromanaging the activities of local
health care organisations and that there are too many centrally
determined targets.

Debates about the desirability of political control of the NHS and the
appropriateness of the Department of Health's role in managing local
providers have raged since its creation. As we shall see there have
been various changes in the interrelationships of the Department

of Health, its ministers and the NHS in the past, although thus far none of these has made the NHS immune to political interference or micromanagement. Reforms implemented since 2002 have dramatically reduced central control by ministers over some NHS providers of health care, and yet accusations of inappropriate political interference continue. Indeed, recent announcements that all hospitals should deep clean their wards (Brown 2007) and all NHS staff should be issued with personal attack alarms (Johnson 2007) suggest that the new Prime Minister and the ministerial team at the Department of Health continue to see it as their role to issue central directives to providers of care. This report examines whether an independent board would address some of these problems with the current governance arrangements and suggests alternative solutions that might address these issues.

The report briefly examines the reasons behind calls for an independent NHS board and presents a number of arguments as to why such proposals should be rejected. These arguments are set in their historical context with a review of the changing relationship between the Department of Health and the NHS. Recent health system reforms are also described, and the bearing that they have on the relationship between the Department of Health and the NHS is discussed. The paper concludes by briefly presenting some alternative suggestions for governing the NHS in future.

Why an independent board?

Proponents of an independent NHS board make a number of arguments as to why greater independence is necessary. Some of these are explicit in public debate and others implicit. We summarise these arguments under two themes: politicisation and micromanagement; for each one we analyse whether an independent board is the answer.

Politicisation

One of the main benefits of an independent NHS board is said to be that it would reduce excessive politicisation of the NHS and create political distance between the NHS and the government.

In its simplest form this argument suggests that politics and the NHS do not mix, and that political interference is at the root of problems experienced by the health care system in this country. If the NHS, and the clinicians working within it, were left alone, the argument goes, things would be better for patients and could be managed more effectively. In particular, the Conservatives have suggested that central targets imposed by politicians have had a damaging effect on the service and that a board would 'ensure that political interference does not result in the distortion of clinical priorities and the denial of autonomy to front-line NHS clinicians' (Conservative Party 2007, p 16).

The problem, however, is that politicisation in this context is ill defined and often regarded as being synonymous with centralisation. Yet the NHS is, and always will be, a party political issue. The NHS/health care was consistently rated as being the most important issue to face Britain since the late 1980s up to 2002, since when issues of defence, crime and race have all been rated as equally important as or more important than health (MORI 2007). Health policy features prominently in party manifestos and is hotly debated in parliament between government and opposition parties and within government.

Nevertheless, critics see politics as being allowed to drive policy, with ideas that were ill thought through being implemented because political commitments had been made. For example, Patricia Hewitt, as Secretary of State, tied her reputation to the achievement of financial balance within the NHS by the end of the financial year 2006/7. She was criticised for prioritising deficit reduction despite the potential negative impact on the quality of patient care. Although some trusts facing financial constraints made compulsory or voluntary redundancies or cut vacant posts, there was only a slight reduction in overall staff numbers and no direct evidence of a deterioration in patient care (Thorlby and Maybin 2007).

Some policies are felt to be ideologically driven rather than evidence based. Indeed, there is a history of policies being developed within the Department of Health and other Whitehall departments under a veil of secrecy, and then implemented without being tested. Calls for evidence-based policy-making suggest that many policies are perceived as political or ideologically driven rather than informed by analysis, modelling or evidence. For example, there is no evidence that a maximum waiting time of 18 weeks for all conditions is either clinically effective or cost effective. Those who favour an independent board argue that it would increase the transparency of decision-making and ensure that decisions were informed by evidence and evaluations.

Another perceived problem is that policy decisions taken by ministers tend to consider short-term benefits. It is argued that an independent NHS board would be able to look ahead over a longer time period than politicians, who do not look beyond the next election. The hope is to enable policy decisions affecting health care to be more strategic and less influenced by the political cycle (Dewar 2003). Political decision-makers are also accused of being more fickle than an appointed board would be – politicians are more likely to react to public opinion and the latest media scandal. Hewitt's intervention in the case of Herceptin, in 2005, provides a stark example of how politicians can be tempted into 'interfering' with health policy in response to media pressure (King's Fund 2005).

Finally, critics point out that the process by which health policy is made has become more politicised. The role of civil servants has diminished and the influence of political advisers has been in the ascendance (Richards and Smith 2002). During the writing of the NHS Plan (Department of Health 2000), the power exercised by the Secretary of State and his advisers was seen to undermine the authority of civil servants and politicise the policy-making process even more. Similarly, the shift in decision-making power across Whitehall, away from the Department of Health towards No 10 and HM Treasury, has also fuelled accusations that health policy has become further politicised.

However, even if the argument of excessive politicisation is accepted, are the advocates of an independent board right to think that this is the answer? It is not clear that this is the case.

First, a board responsible for running the NHS would be subject to intense political pressure. There are always going to be political imperatives driving certain policies and it is hard to see how an independent board would be immune from political intervention.

The fact is that health care will always be a hot political issue, particularly in our tax-funded system, which accounts for 20 per cent of public expenditure at present or 7.8 per cent of the gross domestic product (GDP) (Wanless *et al* 2007). It is not credible that taxpayers or politicians would hand over responsibility for such a large slice of public spending to an unelected body.

Even in countries where health care is predominantly funded from wage-based contributions by employers and employees (as in Germany, the Netherlands and France) or through significant private expenditure (as in the USA), health care is a major political issue. Health reforms in each of these countries have dominated recent electoral campaigns and remain an issue of major public interest. Paul Corrigan, Tony Blair's special adviser on health, was clear that health would always be an issue of electoral interest:

> *The reason [is that] for the last three elections [health] has been a major issue. You can't say to the public stop thinking about it. I cannot see a manifesto saying 'health – nothing to say'. It is just not going to happen.*
> (Triggle 2006)

Andy Burnham's idea was that the objectives for a board could be set and renewed every 10 years, similar to the operation of the BBC Charter. Yet it is difficult to imagine a general election not featuring any commitments on health because the previous government had already been decided on the objectives for the board. The government would therefore have to reserve some powers to intervene or change the board's objectives, thus reintroducing the possibility of politicisation. Furthermore, given the high level of public interest in health care it would be surprising if an independent board could be insulated from political decision-making in response to events, particularly those that were the subject of intense media scrutiny.

Second, an independent board would operate in a highly political environment and would be subject to close scrutiny for bias and vested interest. This will, of course, depend on the composition and constitution of the board. A 'representative' board would be vulnerable to the charge of capture by provider and professional interests. If the board were appointed on a similar basis to other arm's length bodies or executive agencies such as the National Institute for Health and Clinical Excellence (NICE), Monitor and the Healthcare Commission, it might be better placed to resist capture by powerful interest groups and devise policies that were more evidence based. It would then, however, be open to the charge that it was unelected and, to a degree, unaccountable.

Third, there is no reason to assume an independent board would necessarily be any more transparent than the Department of Health. As a public body it would be subject to the Freedom of Information Act, but the amount of information that it would disclose as a matter of routine about its decision-making processes would depend on its constitution and working practices. Transparency should be part of its statutory requirements laid down by government.

Fourth, the ability of the board to act independently and strategically will depend on the ease with which the government could change its objectives and funding allocations, and over what period this was set. There have already been attempts to make longer-term plans with regard to health care funding (three-year comprehensive spending reviews and a commitment on health for five years) and policy (the 10-year NHS Plan). Despite the longer-term funding commitments, local health organisations have seen changes year on year, which continue to make longer-term planning and budgeting difficult. It is not clear that an independent board would behave any differently. Furthermore, if the board were to be given guaranteed funding beyond the three-year Comprehensive Spending Review allocations, other areas of public spending would suffer if the economic situation were not as positive as forecast.

What an independent board might do is create the impression of reduced politicisation that would bring its own benefits, particularly in terms of support by clinicians. Such political distancing could also be beneficial to the public's perception of the NHS. Public opinion surveys show that disenchantment with the government is closely associated with a low opinion of the NHS (Edwards 2007b). It is possible, but by no means certain, that this association could be weakened if the national government were no longer perceived as responsible for running the NHS.

Micromanagement

Micromanagement means direct interference in the day-to-day running of the NHS by ministers. This includes the use of highly specified targets and direct orders by ministers (for example, the sacking of a chief executive).

Although Gordon Brown did not publicly state that there should be independence for the NHS, he did advocate the separation of 'the making of public policy from the independent administration of daily business', and he went on to argue that 'we must now examine how elsewhere we can separate the decisions that in a democracy, elected politicians must take from the business of day-to-day administration' (Brown 2006). Applied to the NHS, this suggests that health policy decisions, where there is a legitimate role for politicians, should continue to be made by ministers, on the advice of civil servants within the Department of Health, although the operational and administrative activities associated with the management of a publicly funded health service should be delegated or devolved. As we see later, the distinction between policy and operational decisions is difficult to apply in practice.

David Cameron, in his speech at the King's Fund last year, said he 'wanted to move away from micromanagement of healthcare' (Cameron 2006). The Conservative Party has consistently argued that the number of centrally dictated targets, the overlapping of different inspection systems and the continuous pressure exerted from the Department of Health (and strategic health authorities (SHAs)) have reduced the degree of independence of NHS managers and put a huge burden on the system (Conservative Party 2003; Hoque *et al* 2004). In its recent proposals the Conservative Party envisages that an independent board would take over responsibility for managing primary care trust (PCT) performance from the Department of Health, but continue to work through SHAs, which would become the 'regional presence' of the board (Conservative Party 2007). They suggest that this would prevent micromanagement by the Department of Health of commissioners and providers.

National targets

The epitome of micromanagement is the setting of highly specified national targets. When it came to power the Labour government adopted and extended the previous Conservative administration's use of national targets as a means of raising standards of care and ensuring the delivery of its key priorities. Failure to achieve these targets had serious consequences for senior managers, and significant effort and resources were channelled into their attainment. There are mixed views on the impact of targets. Although some criticise the selection and implementation of targets for creating perverse behaviours (Bevan and Hood 2006), others suggest that targets and top-down performance management were crucial to the fall in waiting times that has been achieved (Propper *et al* 2007).

Complaints about the current system of performance management concern not only the number of targets but also the type of targets, most of which are focused on process measures. The recent consultation on the outcomes and accountability framework suggests that the Department of Health will retain fewer national targets in future (Department of Health, 2007e). This move was advised by the Public Administration Select Committee (PASC) in 2003 (Public Administration Select Committee 2003), and there have also been subsequent commitments by the Department of Health to reduce the number of national standards and make them more evidence based (Department of Health 2004b, 2005c).

It is therefore clear that steps are being taken already to move to fewer targets with more emphasis on outcomes and less on process. The question again is what more an independent board would be able to achieve. It is expected that the board's objectives would be outcome focused. An independent board would have an agreement or contract of

some sort with the Department of Health as its sponsoring department
(depending on the form of public body), with defined objectives, similar
to public service agreements between the Treasury and the Department
of Health.

The Conservative Party is proposing that the NHS board would use
outcomes rather than process measures, such as waiting times, to
assess the quality and standard of services made available to patients
by PCTs. They argue that this would reduce the damaging effects of
national targets. However, a wholesale switch to outcome measures is
neither feasible nor desirable. First, valid case-mix and risk-adjusted
outcome measures are yet to be developed. Second, given the time lag
between action by the NHS and the impact on outcomes, these
measures would not give timely feedback on the performance of
the NHS.

It is also not clear whether an independent board would be less
involved in direct managerial control or performance management of
the NHS than the Department of Health and SHAs.

As argued below, the creation of foundation trusts has already
significantly reduced the opportunity for the Department of Health to
micromanage the provider side of the NHS. With the conversion of
all NHS providers to foundation trust status by 2009, top-down
performance management by the Department of Health (and SHAs)
will not apply to the delivery side of the NHS from that date.
Micromanagement of providers should therefore diminish without
the need for an independent board. Although managerial control
of providers by the centre has been a major problem since the
mid-1970s, any problems in this area in future are likely to be faced
by commissioners. As Klein (2006, p 262) points out the current reforms
still leave the government directly accountable for PCT performance:

> *While the system of regulation and providers may allow the
> Department to withdraw from direct supervision of providers, and*

intervention in their affairs, it will not absolve it from responsibility for seeing that local purchasers implement national policies effectively.

Would an independent board with the task of overseeing PCTs micromanage less than under the current arrangements?

For some an independent board would at least offer a means by which the commitment to improving health outcomes and reducing health inequalities could be institutionalised – without it, the Department of Health would always be tempted to revert to setting short-term objectives for commissioners. However, it is equally possible that an independent board might be tempted to interfere and translate its strategic objectives based on outcomes into short-term process targets for commissioners. In practice, it does not matter whether commissioners are answerable to an independent board, the Department of Health or independent regulators, there will still need to be a greater focus on health outcomes and population health.

At this stage in their development, it may be appropriate for PCTs to receive significant levels of support, particularly where capacity is weakest. Currently this 'support' or guidance is provided centrally by the Department of Health and SHAs. Under the commissioning framework (Department of Health 2007d) it is expected that PCTs will also contract with private companies to provide commissioning support. An independent board with responsibility for commissioning would be under the same obligations to support PCTs, at least initially, until their capacity developed sufficiently for them to operate more autonomously. If there is a tendency for the centre to overdo this and turn support into micromanagement, there is no reason to believe that a board would be any less prone to this than the Department of Health.

Andy Burnham, Minister of State, despite having been an early enthusiast for an independent board, later ruled out the idea on these very grounds:

*The era of the top-down, centrally driven target is coming to an end.
An independent, central board running the NHS would replicate the
same top-down approach but with less accountable people running
the NHS.*
(Revill 2007)

In reality the extent to which commissioners need to be supported, or
indeed micromanaged, may depend more on the pace of improvement
by PCTs than on whether they are accountable to the Department of
Health (via SHAs) or an independent board. The answer probably lies
in developing a model of 'earned autonomy'.

Reorganisation

Proponents of an independent board also expect it to reduce one of the
most damaging aspects of central government control – continuous
structural reforms. Gwyn Bevan (2006, p 252) vividly describes the
permanent revolution in the NHS since New Labour came to power:

*The Department of Health has been reorganised three times; the
regional structure and purchasing tier in the NHS have each been
reorganised four times; there have been mergers of providers of
acute services and reorganisation of mental health services; and
inspectorates have been created, expanded, abolished and merged
(with one lasting 17 days). The policy of a market driven by provider
competition in which money followed the patient was introduced in
1991, abolished in 1997, and reintroduced from 2006, after a five
year interregnum during which the NHS was subjected to annual
star ratings, a Soviet-style regime of targets backed by sanctions
and rewards.*

These reorganisations have certainly caused major upheaval for
professionals, staff and organisations, diverting attention away from
operational issues with very little evidence that the benefits have
outweighed the costs. For example, the re-structuring of PCTs and SHAs
in 2006 resulted in large-scale redeployment of staff and redundancies,
particularly of managerial staff. A further proposed reorganisation of

PCTs into commissioning-only organisations (Department of Health 2005b) was partially retracted when the level of opposition from NHS community staff and the scale of disruption were recognised.

There is anecdotal evidence that NHS staff associate unwanted changes at a local level with government policy, so they are generally supportive of proposals to hand over decisions to an independent body. It is perhaps not surprising therefore that the British Medical Association (BMA) has come out in favour of an independent board that, it claims, would 'separate national politics from the day to day running of the NHS' (BMA 2007, p 12). For many staff, the 'permanent revolution' inspired by politicians and implemented by the Department of Health is precisely the approach that an independent board would avoid.

Certainly a board would find it more difficult to push through major restructuring that required primary or secondary legislation. However, it would not be prevented from changing the number or size of PCTs or SHAs. It might also be more risk averse and conservative, and therefore more likely to preserve the status quo. Even with the existence of a board, presumably parliament could vote through a Bill to reorganise the NHS so there is no guarantee that the creation of an independent board would avoid reorganisation. At most it might make the life of busy reformers more difficult. In the medium term, however, the difference would be minimal because all the main political parties have vowed not to embark on another reorganisation for the foreseeable future.

Focus on public health

Another possible advantage of taking management responsibility for the NHS away from the Department of Health is that it might free up civil servants and the Secretary of State to focus more on public health. For Dewar (2003, p 1), an NHS agency:

> ...could enable government to broaden its horizons, away from a preoccupation with accountability for each and every action within the NHS, towards a more general concern for the impact of poverty, environment, food, housing and education on health.

This is also central to the Conservative Party (2007) proposals that include a complete separation of public health from health care. It is true that currently the Secretary of State for Health is more often blamed for failures in the NHS than for a deterioration in the public's health. If accountability for access, quality and cost-effectiveness of health services was transferred to an independent board, the Conservatives argue that this would allow a greater focus on public health by the Department of Health. However, it is not clear how far this would go. The idea that the Department of Health would not have any role in health care policy and that all decisions would be left to a board is not tenable. It is difficult to imagine where the line would be drawn. For example, no government would allow a board to introduce top-up vouchers for health care or health savings accounts. However, would a decision to move to local pay within the NHS be considered an operational matter and therefore for the board rather than elected politicians to decide?

It is hard to see how a strategy for improving public health would succeed if it were not well co-ordinated with the structures within the health care system. Health care makes a significant contribution to public health through primary and secondary prevention such as prescribing statins and smoking cessation treatments. Given the prevalence of chronic diseases and risk factors such as smoking and obesity, it will be increasingly important for health care services to support and encourage patients to change health behaviour.

Furthermore, the complexity of many contemporary health issues means that there should be a co-ordinated approach involving personal health services and wider public health measures. The NHS locally can do, and does, much to promote health and prevent illness both on its own and working in partnership with others. There would be a danger that, if public health and health care were separated at the national and strategic level by the creation of an independent board, this might weaken the incentives for co-operation on health improvement locally. On the other hand, there may be ways to prevent this – for example, the board could be charged with ensuring that NHS commissioners co-operate at a local level with existing public health structures and deliver against agreed public health targets.

Summary

Although an independent board is advocated on the basis that it will avoid politicisation and reduce micromanagement, there are a number of reasons why a board may not necessarily achieve these objectives. In the next section, we examine how these issues have played out in the past. To what extent were these problems present in the NHS in the past? And, if they were, how were they addressed?

The evolution of political and managerial control of the NHS

It is not our intention to repeat accounts of the historical development of the Department of Health and the NHS. These can be read elsewhere (Day and Klein 1997; Ham 2004). In this section we highlight how the relationships between ministers and the NHS, and between the Department of Health (and its predecessors) and the NHS, have changed.

Local management autonomy

When the NHS was set up in 1948 as a health service centrally funded by general taxation, it was clear to Aneurin Bevan that the NHS should be accountable to politicians. As Bevan himself put it at the time, 'if a bedpan is dropped on a hospital floor in Tredegar, its noise should resound in the Palace of Westminster' (cited in Nairne 1984, p 34). And in another less frequently cited quote: 'Every time a maid kicks over a bucket of slops in a ward an agonized wail will go through Whitehall' (cited in Timmins 1995).

The vision of the 'dropped bedpan' has since been used to illustrate the problems of excessive ministerial interference and central control by the Department of Health. Yet, at the time these words were uttered, ministers had only weak control over the providers of care. The NHS Act 1946 changed the funding arrangements and the ownership status of hospitals, but not the organisational structure.

The Ministry of Health was created only in 1919, health having been primarily the responsibility of local government boards until that time (Rayner 1994). Even after nationalisation, in 1948, hospitals continued to enjoy significant freedom. Until 1974, teaching hospitals (which had been voluntary hospitals) remained under the management of a board of governors that reported to the Ministry of Health. Other hospitals were managed by hospital management committees (HMCs), the members of which were appointed by regional hospital boards (RHBs); these, in turn, were appointed by the Minister of Health. According to Rayner (1994), the authority of the 15 regional health boards was weak at this stage relative to the authority of the management committees.

The Ministry of Health initially continued to function in the way that it was used to, that is, setting policy. Day and Klein (1997) likened the relationship between the Minister of Health and the regional health boards in the 1950s and 1960s to that between a 'weak Persian emperor' and the 'Persian satraps' (following a metaphor used by Richard Crossman).

During this period NHS providers continued to enjoy significant autonomy and the Ministry of Health and politicians appear to have had little ability to intervene directly in the operation of the NHS. The creation of foundation trusts could be seen as an attempt to return hospitals to the control of local boards or committees, a position that many of them enjoyed until the mid-1970s.

Regionalisation

Over time the Ministry of Health increasingly sought to ensure the implementation of its policy to attain national consistency. As Rayner (1994, p 29) describes:

> When the Ministry first acquired responsibilities for the Health Service in 1948 it was essentially a policy department. With experience it became appreciated that policies were all very well but not worth much unless executed by the NHS authorities. Over the years, the department acquired an increasing facility to make inter-authority comparisons, showing wide variations in the use of resources. It thus became increasingly apparent that some means was needed to ensure that the actions of field authorities were acceptable.

The NHS Reorganisation Act of 1973 heralded significant changes in the relationships between NHS providers and the Department of Health. These followed the recommendations of a report from McKinsey and were implemented in 1974.

NHS providers were brought into a more hierarchical relationship with lines of authority running up to the Secretary of State. Ninety area health authorities (AHAs) were created, which had direct managerial authority over both hospitals (including teaching hospitals) and community health services, as well as joint planning responsibilities with local authorities. Beneath the area health authorities were district management teams, which managed hospitals and family practitioner committees (FPCs) that took responsibility for administering contracts for GPs, dentists, pharmacists and opticians. AHAs were under the supervision of 14 regional health authorities (RHAs). Regional health authorities held more power than their predecessors and as statutory bodies were more insulated from politics.

Dissatisfaction and criticism of the more centrally controlled system quickly emerged. The Merrison Royal Commission, set up in 1976 to examine the best use and management of the financial and personnel resources in the NHS, criticised the 'bedpan' politics of the NHS that ministerial accountability had created (Royal Commission 1979). According to Day and Klein (1997, p 6), 'the report recommended that formal responsibility for the delivery of services, including accountability to parliament, should be transferred to the regional health authorities'. This was rejected as unconstitutional (Rayner 1994). At this time the idea of an independent health commission or board was also considered but not 'endorsed' (Day and Klein 1997).

Further changes in 1982 aimed to strengthen the autonomy of district health authorities (DHAs) (which replaced area health authorities) vis-à-vis regional health authorities and the Department of Health. Concerns were raised, however, by the Public Administration Select

Committee and resulted in a system of regional accountability reviews in which regional health authorities were expected to answer to the Department of Health for the implementation of major departmental policies by district health authorities and for the region's efficiency in the use of resources. To satisfy the Department of Health, the regional health authorities needed similarly to be in a position to call their district health authorities to account, and the result of these processes was to put the regions into a stronger position in relation to their field authorities (Rayner 1994).

So, although proposals to strengthen regional and district authorities were intended to reduce central control, concerns about accountability for public spending meant that these structures were used to implement stricter systems of monitoring and performance management by the Department of Health.

Regional structures of the NHS have continued to focus on implementation of national policy priorities. In 1996, the 14 regional health authorities were replaced by eight NHS executive regional offices of the Department of Health, and the district health authorities and the family health service authorities (FHSAs) were merged to form health authorities. The regional offices were seen to 'occupy an important position in the chain of accountability from the local level to the centre' (European Observatory Healthcare Systems 1999, p 14). They were responsible for the regional implementation of national policy and monitoring the performance of health authorities.

The separation of policy formulation and implementation

In the 1980s and 1990s the solution to the problem of ministerial control and the involvement of civil servants in the management of the NHS was to try to separate responsibilities for policy formulation and policy implementation.

In 1983, Sir Roy Griffiths, a managing director of a chain of supermarkets, chaired a review into the management of the NHS, which stemmed from concerns that the NHS was not managerially effective and reflected a belief in the superior efficiency of the private sector (Griffiths 1983). Griffiths proposed new boards at the national level with separate responsibilities for policy and strategic planning, and operational management. These were the Supervisory Board and the Management Board respectively. The Supervisory Board's role was to set objectives for the NHS, take strategic decisions and monitor performance (Day and Klein 1997). The Supervisory Board was renamed the Policy Board in 1989 but was largely irrelevant, did not meet frequently and was eventually abandoned.

The Management Board assumed responsibility for implementation of policies, and was expected to provide leadership to the management of the NHS and control performance (Griffiths 1983). The report recommended that only a small management body was needed at the centre to manage the NHS so that 'responsibility is pushed as far down the line as possible, i.e. to the point where action can be taken effectively' (Griffiths 1983, p 2). Rather than propose that the Management Board be set up as an independent corporation that would require legislative change, Griffiths proposed a model whereby the Board remained within the Department of Health.

Reducing ministerial involvement in the management of the NHS proved difficult (Day and Klein 1997). In fact the Management Board never achieved much distance from ministerial interest. This may in part result from the fact that the Management Board was never set up to be legislatively separate from the Department of Health, as current advocates of an independent board would envisage. Alternatively, it may simply reflect the fact that the way policies are implemented is also political and therefore the separation between policy and operational matters will always be difficult, whatever the institutional separation.

The Management Board was renamed the NHS Management Executive in 1989 and was given significant responsibilities. The changes precipitated a creeping colonisation of the Department of Health by

NHS managers, a legacy that is still evident in the make-up of those occupying senior positions in the Department of Health today (Greer and Jarman 2007). The introduction of general management into the NHS shifted power away from independently minded professionals and introduced a more corporate approach, under which central demands were more likely to be followed.

In 1992, the Functions and Manpower Review team considered further strengthening the separation of management and policy by either creating an independent corporation or transforming the Management Executive into an agency. These proposals were never implemented because they were perceived to undermine the process of parliamentary accountability (Department of Health 1993; Day and Klein 2000).

By the time of the Banks review into the organisation of the Department of Health in 1994, ministers had decided that the top management of the NHS should remain 'an integral part of the Department of Health, albeit a very special part with its own style and identity' (Banks 1994, p 11). The Banks review recommended that the NHS Executive should be responsible for 'all aspects of health services policy work, and policy and implementation' (Banks 1994, p14). The report stated that 'policy and implementation must be as closely aligned as possible' (Banks 1994, summary 8.ii). Day and Klein (1997, p 15) saw the Banks report as 'an obituary of the notion that policy and management could be separated'. Banks (1994, p i) argued that the management of health care could not be separated from politics because of the need for public accountability:

The degree of public and Parliamentary interest in health and social services matters is high, but responding to this interest is in no way optional. It is an essential feature of a democratic political system that Ministers and through them, the Department, should be able to be held to account for huge sums of public money, whose spending has implications at some time or another for the health and well-being of every person in the country.

Policy formulation and implementation were firmly consolidated in 2000 when the NHS Executive was effectively abolished and the posts of Permanent Secretary and Chief Executive were merged. Nigel Crisp held this joint position from October 2000 until his resignation in March 2006. During this period the major focus of the Department of Health and its officials was on delivery of a policy agenda, not only set out by ministers but also heavily influenced by the Prime Minister and his advisers.

The creation of an NHS Executive or Management Board *within* the Department of Health meant that the division between policy formulation and policy implementation was never realised and the separation was easily reversed. Recent changes in the Department of Health are attempting to recreate this internal division. After Sir Nigel Crisp's departure, the posts of NHS Chief Executive and Departmental Permanent Secretary were again split. David Nicholson was appointed as the former and Hugh Taylor as the latter.

Proposals to create a separate management executive within the Department of Health, with its own structures and directors (including a medical director separate from the chief medical officer), were formally announced on 9 May 2007 in a written statement. The reorganisation was set in the context of the capability review then under way at the Department of Health (Cabinet Office 2007). The reorganisation reflects three core but distinct aspects of the Department of Health: a department of state, the headquarters of the NHS, and the body responsible for setting policy on public health corresponding to the posts of Permanent Secretary, Chief Executive of the NHS and Chief Medical Officer. Although these changes currently constitute no more than an internal reorganisation, there has been speculation that the NHS Executive team is a forerunner to an independent board (Carvel 2007). This now seems unlikely under the current government but these changes reflect a continuing desire to separate out the business of government and that of the NHS.

Summary

This historical analysis has shown how the relationships between the NHS and the Department of Health and its ministers have changed over time. Contemporary concerns about excessive politicisation and micromanagement have been present in past discussions about the NHS, at least since the 1970s. Before 1974 providers of care continued to enjoy significant autonomy. The Ministry of Health was a relatively weak player, focused on policy.

Subsequent reforms that strengthened regional and local tiers of the NHS also created a hierarchical management structure, which allowed the Department of Health and its ministers to exert greater control. Later reforms tried to address the problems created by 'bedpan' politics but they failed to reduce the involvement of the centre in local management. For example, although the Griffiths reforms aimed to support enhanced local management, in reality the creation of an NHS Management Board within the Department of Health strengthened central control. The creation of the Management Board and its successor, the NHS Management Executive, were also attempts to separate policy formulation and management, but ministerial involvement in day-to-day management reasserted itself. We can only speculate as to whether the outcomes would have been different had the Executive been given greater independence.

A number of reviews into the management of the NHS considered the possibility of creating an independent agency or board to manage the NHS. The idea was rejected for a number of reasons – such changes would need primary legislation, challenge the requirements of public accountability and diminish ministerial authority. In the next section, we consider how current reforms to the NHS are changing the relationships between the Department of Health and the NHS and between ministers and the NHS, and reflect on the implications for proposals for an independent board.

Independence in the context of current NHS reforms

The idea of handing over responsibility for the management of the NHS from the Department of Health to an independent board or agency has as its premise the belief that decision-making authority is still held almost entirely by the Department of Health and its ministers. Recent reforms, however, have created a plethora of independent and semi-autonomous organisations that are not controlled directly from the Department of Health. The NHS is now characterised by greater diversity on the supply side, including autonomous NHS providers, greater individual choice of providers by patients, devolved responsibility for commissioning and delegated responsibility for regulation. Overall, the picture is a great deal more complex. The potential role of an independent board and its impact on the NHS needs to be examined in this context.

Autonomous providers

The Labour government pushed through controversial legislation to create foundation trusts. There were 77 foundation trusts at 1 October 2007 (Monitor 2007). The government's objective is for all acute, specialist and mental health trusts to have applied for foundation status by 2008.

Foundation trusts were created as public benefit corporations, a bespoke form of public ownership, which means that they were no longer under the direction of the Secretary of State but required in law to use their assets to promote their primary purpose of providing NHS services (Department of Health 2005a). Consequently, problems in these hospitals are no longer the subject of parliamentary questions. They have greater operational and financial freedoms, for example, to borrow money for investment (within constraints set by Monitor) and to set the terms and conditions for their staff. It is no longer possible for the Department of Health to issue management directives to these providers; however, they do have to meet the core standards as assessed by the Healthcare Commission and set down by the Department of Health. Instead, foundation trusts are accountable to their councils of governors made up of elected members (representing the public, patients and staff) and appointed governors (representing PCTs, local authorities and other local organisations). Monitor is the independent regulator of NHS foundation trusts. It is responsible for authorising them and making sure that they operate within the terms of authorisation, monitoring financial performance and intervening in cases of significant problems.

The private and voluntary sectors have an increasing role to play in providing services to NHS-funded patients. The Department of Health made contracts with the first wave of independent sector treatment centres (ISTCs), but has indicated that future contracts will be led by PCTs. These providers of elective treatment are included in the list that is made available to patients when choosing where they want to be referred to (Department of Health 2007a). The government expects that up to 157 other private sector facilities will be included in the extended choice network in future. Commissioners will be expected to reimburse these providers at the national tariff when patients choose them under 'free choice' from April 2008.

Currently, most primary and community care staff are employed by PCTs (except GPs on General Medical Service (GMS) contracts). The government announced, and then subsequently retracted, the decision that PCTs should divest themselves of this responsibility, which would be very difficult to implement because of staff resistance. However, it is likely that some form of NHS primary and community trust will be created that may either gain foundation status in its own right or merge with an acute trust to create a vertically integrated delivery system. Although it is already possible to bring private providers into the primary care sector, so far few PCTs have made use of these arrangements (Walsh *et al* 2007). In an effort to increase the responsiveness of primary care and to deliver the improvements in access and quality of services, the government has recently urged PCTs to open more primary and community services to competitive tender in future (Department of Health 2007f).

The creation of a mixed economy of care, including autonomous public providers, and private and voluntary sector providers, means that the Department of Health will have diminishing direct control over health care providers. Direct managerial control is being replaced by other forms of accountability such as contractual accountability to PCTs, local accountability to overview and scrutiny committees, and regulatory accountability to the new health and social care regulator.

These policies are unlikely to be reversed, at least in the short term. The independence from the Department of Health currently enjoyed by public providers of health services is likely to continue, as will the role of the private and voluntary sector in the provision of health services. It remains to be seen whether the level of autonomy enjoyed by local hospitals in the early years of the NHS can be re-created. It will depend in part on the fate of NHS hospitals that are unlikely to attain foundation status, for which there is currently no clear failure regime. It also requires the Department of Health to acknowledge explicitly that operational issues are matters for local management. Current policies, if fully implemented, at least reduce, if not eliminate, micromanagement of providers by the Department of Health. An independent board may therefore not be justified on these grounds.

Devolved commissioning

Primary care trusts are now responsible for 80 per cent of NHS spending – equivalent to around £58 billion (King's Fund 2006). Since October 2006 there have been 152 PCTs (reduced from 303), which each cover an average population of just under 300,000. Most PCTs are commissioners as well as providers of primary and community care. As commissioners, they are responsible for agreeing contracts with a range of providers to ensure access to services for the local population.

Although PCTs are public bodies and directly accountable to the Department of Health, they do have significant discretion over how they allocate resources. They are able to determine local purchasing policies (within the constraints of guidance published by the National Institute for Health and Clinical Excellence (NICE), make important resource allocation decisions and set clinical thresholds for accessing care (for example, thresholds at which referrals for treatment are made). Analysis of programme budgeting data shows that even after adjusting for need there are significant variations in the level of PCT spending on different clinical areas (King's Fund 2006). PCTs are currently not required to justify these variations.

In theory at least, local commissioners have a great deal of freedom to decide how to allocate funds. There is almost no ring fencing of funds and, even where money is earmarked, such as the sums associated with implementation of the public health White Paper *Choosing Health* (Department of Health 2004a), there is some evidence that they can be diverted elsewhere in that case to reduce deficits and meet productivity targets (Chief Medical Officer 2005). PCTs are not under any statutory obligation to comply with NICE guidance, although this is expected and some monitoring of compliance is carried out.

Under the new framework contract (Department of Health 2007d), PCTs can contract with the private sector for commissioning support, which can either be for discrete functions such as data analysis or needs assessment, or cover the whole commissioning process (called end-to-end commissioning). Other than the checks undertaken by the Department of Health for these organisations to be included on the framework contract, they are not subject to any further financial regulations or inspections. Private commissioning companies will be held to account via a contract with the PCT board.

Many of the proposals for an independent board explicitly see it having a function to oversee commissioning. Some of the roles envisaged for the board, such as defining a package of core NHS benefits, in effect remove responsibility from local commissioners, thus recentralising authority. On the other hand, more explicit national commissioning rules might reduce unjustified variations. A board would also mean that PCTs were no longer directly accountable to ministers; instead through the board they would be accountable to either the sponsoring government department or to parliament (depending on its constitution).

Arm's length bodies

Many of the roles and responsibilities once in the purview of the Department of Health have been handed over to arm's length bodies, creating a new regulatory landscape for the NHS (Lewis *et al* 2006). The Department of Health is no longer the sole, or indeed main, source of rules or regulations that govern the behaviour of NHS organisations. These regulatory bodies enjoy various degrees of independence (Figure 1) and therefore they are less subject to interference by

FIGURE 1: EXTENT OF INDEPENDENCE OF DIFFERENT PUBLIC BODIES

Part of Department of Health			Independent
Executive agencies NHS Purchasing and Supply Agency, Medicine and Healthcare Products Regulatory Agency	**NHS bodies** PCTs	**Non-departmental public bodies** *Advisory* NICE *Tribunals* Care Standards Tribunal *Executive* Healthcare Commission, Monitor	**Public corporations**

Source: (Cabinet Office 2006; Edwards 2007a).

ministers than if their functions were carried out by the Department of Health directly.

For example, the Healthcare Commission, Commission for Social Care Inspection, Health Protection Agency and Monitor enjoy significant independence in carrying out their functions. They are executive non-departmental public bodies (NDBPs), of which there are a total of nine in the area of health, so while they are sponsored by the Department of Health they are formally accountable to parliament. There are also advisory non-departmental public bodies (33 in health), including NICE, the Commission for Patient and Public Involvement in Health, Gene Therapy Advisory Committee and Doctors' and Dentists' Review Body, and tribunal non-departmental public bodies that include the FSHA authority, the Mental Health Review Tribunal and the Care Standards Tribunal.

In contrast, the Medicines and Healthcare products and Regulatory Agency (MHRA) and the NHS Purchasing and Supply Agency are executive agencies. These are part of ministerial departments and have a quasi-contractual relationship with them. The minister has formal control and the staff are employed by the civil service.

A review of the Department of Health's arm's lengths bodies in 2004 proposed reducing the number from 38 to 20 (Department of Health 2004c). As a consequence, the government has merged a number of them – for example, the functions of the Health Development Agency have been transferred to NICE. The government is committed to merging the Healthcare Commission with the Commission for Social Care Inspection and the Mental Health Act Commission in 2008. This will create a new, single regulator of health and social care (Department of Health 2006c). A Bill on this was introduced on 15 November 2007. In the latest directory of public bodies, published by the Cabinet Office on 31 March 2006, there were a total of 68 public bodies sponsored by the Department of Health (Cabinet Office 2006). Although the government is committed to reducing the size and number of regulatory bodies, it is likely that these bodies will retain important responsibilities and a significant degree of independence in how they carry them out.

A transparent system of rules is important for the effective functioning of a mixed economy of health care providers, where the independent and third sectors compete alongside publicly owned providers for patients and commissioning contracts. New providers want the rules governing the emerging health care market to be explicit and consistently applied in order to have some confidence in business plans. It is possible that an independent board could, as in other regulated industries, take decisions about price regulation and enforcement of competition rules. An increasing number of these rules are set by independent regulators (although there is potential for further delegation as discussed in the final section of this paper).

It is not clear at present whether it is envisaged that a board would replace existing regulators, thus further reducing their number, or whether it would operate alongside them. This partly arises out of confusion between performance management and performance assessment. It is perfectly possible for the board to be responsible for performance management of NHS commissioners, but for assessment to be carried out by another independent body. Proposals need to be clear as to the desirability of separating out performance management from performance assessment.

Summary

Changes in the health care system over recent years have diminished the need for an independent board. Providers are more autonomous and managerially independent than in the past. Commissioners enjoy a significant amount of discretion in decision-making but remain accountable for public spending nationally. Regulators have varying degrees of authority and independence to carry out their functions and responsibilities. To some extent current reforms are beginning to address the problems of excessive political interference and central managerial control identified by the proponents of an independent board.

Although current reforms to the NHS mean that there are fewer control levers in the hands of ministers, and in some ways it is more difficult to impose change from the centre, there remains the possibility that ministerial control will be re-established. Given this danger, we suggest that other changes may be needed to secure local autonomy and prevent excessive central control of health services in future.

Alternatives to an independent board

In this paper so far we have reviewed the arguments for creating an independent board. On the whole we have not found them convincing. At the heart of these debates there appears to be a fundamental concern about the excessive power of the executive. The debates in health probably reflect wider concerns across government about the demise of Cabinet government, the undermining of parliamentary authority and the rise in the role of special advisers. Rather than try to depoliticise health policy by handing power over from ministers and the Department of Health to an independent board, we suggest below a number of alternative ways of addressing the problems of excessive politicisation and micromanagement, which could ensure that in the future decisions about health policy are more transparent, strategic and focused on outcomes:

■ adopt the principle of subsidiarity
■ strengthen the role of parliament
■ redefine the 'bedpan' doctrine
■ strengthen local accountability
■ increase transparency
■ create an NHS constitution.

Adopt the principle of subsidiarity

To protect the health service from excessive central control, we suggest that, rather than create another central authority in the form of an independent board, the Department of Health should adopt the principle of subsidiarity. This would ensure that government delegates as much responsibility locally as is appropriate.

Subsidiarity is a familiar term in the context of the European Union. It defines the relationship between the European Community and member states. Article 5 of the Treaty Establishing the European Community requires that the Community take action 'only if and in so far as the objectives of the proposed action cannot be sufficiently achieved by the member states and can therefore, by reason of the scale or effects of the proposed action, be better achieved by the Community' (European Community 2002). In the EU, the principle has come to mean that action should be taken at national or sub-national levels whenever possible (Nugent 1999).

The application of the principle of subsidiarity to health policy in England should mean not that every decision be made locally, but where to do so would enable objectives to be effectively achieved. Some decisions and actions might remain national – for example, decisions about the standard requirements for an IT platform could be set nationally, but the procurement and delivery of an IT infrastructure could be devolved to local organisations as long as they met minimum compatibility requirements. By assessing every decision or action currently taken by the Department of Health against this principle, it would help to clarify which ones could best be delegated and which could more appropriately be retained or made nationally. It is unclear at present how such a principle could be enacted. The idea needs to be considered as part of the discussions about broader constitutional reform.

If it were determined that responsibility should be retained at a national level, then another rule would be needed to guide the decision where possible to delegate to an arm's length body or regulator. Here it is more difficult. A range of independent national bodies has taken on functions that in the past would have been within the remit of the Department of Health, and yet it retains several functions and responsibilities that might benefit from greater independence. Here we briefly discuss those about which there has been recent debate: service reconfiguration, resource allocation, tariff, and pay and conditions. Interestingly, both resource allocation and pay negotiation have been identified in the past as tasks that should be delegated to an NHS agency (Dewar 2003).

Service reconfigurations

Under section 38 of the Local Government Act 2000, local authority overview and scrutiny committees (OSC) have been given powers to scrutinise health services provided or commissioned by NHS bodies and refer contested decisions on service closures or reconfigurations to the Secretary of State (Department of Health 2003). The Secretary of State may refer cases to the independent reconfiguration panel, which has a purely advisory role. Few cases have been referred to the panel or decided in this way (Day and Klein 2007). By strengthening the powers of the reconfiguration panel and giving it even greater independence, it may be possible to remove politicians from decisions about local service reconfigurations.

As Patricia Hewitt suggested (Hewitt 2007), the panel could be separated from government by allowing overview and scrutiny committees to refer a proposal directly to it rather than through the Secretary of State. Second, the panel's current advisory role could be changed to make its decisions binding. In addition, the Secretary of State's current right of veto could be removed, as the Institute for Public Policy Research (IPPR) has proposed (Farrington-Douglas and Brooks 2007). It is less clear how strategic decisions about reconfigurations will or should be made. Could an independent panel be given greater scope to determine the strategic shape of reconfigurations?

Following the principle of subsidiarity, two scenarios are possible: one is that the strategic vision for service configuration is set by SHAs and realised through the commissioning intentions of PCTs; the other is that choice and competition are allowed to shape the market, although in this case national regulations governing mergers and acquisitions, anti-competitive behaviour, new entrants and failing providers will be as important in mediating the impact of competition on the shape of service provision.

The government's wide-ranging review of the NHS and the appointment of Professor Lord Darzi as Minister of Health, following his review of health services in London (Healthcare for London 2006), suggest that the government intends to develop plans for how local health services should be organised (Thorlby *et al* 2007). At this stage it is not clear whether reconfiguration will be subject to national guidelines or whether there will be locally determined models. At a local level there is a further issue as to whether changes will be planned or commissioners will allow patient choice and payment by results to create the momentum for change.

Resource allocation

As long as we continue to fund health care from general taxation, it is unlikely that resource allocation will be anything other than nationally determined. Resource allocation and the formula used to allocate health care funds locally have been based on a transparent formula since the Resource Allocation Working Party (RAWP) was formed in the 1970s. The formula proposed then, and the revisions made since, have sought to allocate resources to reflect health needs. Currently resources are allocated to PCTs according to a formula devised by York University (called the Allocation of Resources to English Areas (AREA) formula) (Sutton *et al* 2002).

Even though the funds are allocated by the Department of Health, they are allocated in line with the recommendations of the Advisory Committee on Resource Allocation (ACRA), which was established in 1997 and is made up of appointed members (approved by the Department of Health's Director of Finance, and the chair of ACRA) (Hansard 2006). Despite there being no evidence that the current arrangements for determining the resource allocation formula are politicised, Patricia Hewitt, when Secretary of State for Health, suggested that ACRA might be given even greater independence from the Department of Health (Hewitt 2007). Although the idea was not elaborated on, we might imagine ACRA being given authority to determine the resource allocation rather than merely to advise. Perhaps by ensuring that the membership of ACRA is independently appointed, and its technical calculations and recommendations are seen to be made independently of government, public trust in the process could be enhanced.

Yet there will always be an element of political judgement involved. The objectives for which the allocation formula is designed – that is, equity of access to services – or reducing health inequalities are value-based judgements and would be difficult for any government to delegate. There currently appears to be some disagreement between the political parties on this issue: should the formula reflect underlying health needs that may not be expressed with the aim of reducing inequalities in health, or should it above all ensure equal access to health care services and respond to expressed need? For example, is it right to allocate more to areas where there are large numbers of older people, but which are more affluent, or to allocate more to deprived areas where demand is less but underlying need may be greater?

Price setting

Currently the setting of prices (in the form of the national tariff under Payment by Results) is undertaken by the Department of Health, largely based on average cost data submitted by NHS providers. To date the government has not chosen explicitly to set prices normatively in order to send price signals to payers/providers (for example, to encourage use of less invasive techniques). As the mechanisms for directly controlling providers wither away, the use of regulatory tools such as price setting may become a more important instrument to influence providers. Price setting is a powerful regulatory tool used in other regulated industries. The government is therefore likely to want to maintain some influence over the mechanism by which the price is established, but it is important that the process should be transparent and based on independently validated data. The technical work to gather cost information and calculate the tariff based on average costs or best practice patient pathways (or bundles) could be given to or overseen by an independent body similar to ACRA.

Pay and conditions

The Department of Health has reduced its direct involvement in negotiating the national pay and conditions for NHS staff. In 2004 it set up NHS Employers under the auspices of the NHS Confederation to negotiate pay and conditions. They lead contract negotiations on behalf of employers with both independent contractors in primary care (for example, GMS and the community pharmacy contract), and health care professionals employed in the NHS. Since 2005 they have also submitted evidence to the independent pay review bodies on behalf of employers (NHS Employers 2007).

It is not clear how effective the decision to remove negotiations of pay and terms and conditions from the Department of Health has been, because agreements on Agenda for Change, and the consultants' contract pre-date the establishment of NHS Employers. Evaluations of these new contracts suggest that they have not yet delivered the anticipated improvements in productivity and patient care (Williams and Buchan 2006; Buchan and Evans 2007). It is not clear if political pressure and ministerial intervention meant that the UK health departments foreclosed on an agreement with employee and employer representatives (the NHS Confederation), although they knew that the contracts offered limited value for money.

Application of the principle of subsidiarity might suggest that the responsibility for pay and conditions could be further devolved to local organisations. Although foundation trusts in theory have the ability to break with national contracts, to date none has chosen to do so. Local pay may appear to have advantages in creating a more flexible pay system, but any changes require the support of local (and often highly unionised) staff. Unless the deal on offer was better than that negotiated nationally, it is very unlikely that staff would agree to depart from the nationally agreed contracts. It seems likely then that, for the foreseeable future, there will continue to be national (but somewhat depoliticised) negotiation of pay and conditions for NHS staff.

Discussion

Application of the principle of subsidiarity also requires an assessment of whether objectives can still be achieved by pushing decision-making to the lowest possible level. There may be some roles that are most effectively discharged nationally, such as the negotiation of pay and conditions, as a result of the presence of strong nationally organised unions, or coverage decisions because of public support for geographical equity of access. Currently, price setting, and pay and resource allocation are nationally determined whereas reconfiguration is local (with recourse to national adjudication) and coverage decisions are also local (within the context of national guidance from NICE). The principle of subsidiarity could help guide the government to establish the right balance between central and local decision-making.

A number of responsibilities are already discharged by independent bodies such as NICE and NHS Employers. There may, however, be potential on the part of the Department of Health and ministers for further delegation of a number of decisions such as those concerning local reconfigurations, resource allocation and price setting. Even if these functions were delegated to independent bodies, their work would need to be informed by policy objectives. There must be a distinction between purely technical decisions and those that require value-based judgements. So, for example, while the technical work to determine resource allocation could be delegated, the objectives underpinning resource allocation are essentially political. Setting the goals, standards and priorities for organisations with delegated responsibilities will probably remain a matter for government and those who are democratically elected.

By applying the principle of subsidiarity, health policy decision-making could become more strategic. The Department of Health would be freer to focus on fewer policy issues, to establish priorities and objectives for other bodies and to set the framework within which local organisations such as commissioners operate. It would provide a basis for determining which functions the Department of Health should retain and where devolution and delegation are appropriate.

Strengthen the role of parliament

Proposals for an independent board are designed to reduce ministerial interference in the running of the health service. Yet, under most of the proposed schemes, the board would be accountable to ministers. We suggest that a more effective counterweight to ministerial interference would be strengthened parliamentary accountability.

Parliament has an important role in holding government and its ministers to account, examining and challenging the work of government, ensuring that ministers behave properly and public resources are spent appropriately. Accountability is achieved through a number of mechanisms: oral and written questions, departmental question times, debates, scrutiny of Bills and select committee hearings. The main committees that scrutinise health policy are the Health Committee and the Public Accounts Committee.

The Health Committee is appointed by the House of Commons 'to examine the expenditure, administration and policy of the Department of Health and its associated bodies'. Its constitution and powers are set out in House of Commons Standing Order No 152 (United Kingdom Parliament 2007b). Recent and current issues examined by the Health Committee include public health, NHS finance, public and patient involvement, and workforce planning.

The Public Accounts Committee is appointed to examine 'the accounts showing the appropriation of the sums granted by Parliament to meet the public expenditure, and of such other accounts laid before Parliament as the committee may think fit' (Standing Order No 148 (United Kingdom Parliament 2007a)). In the first half of 2007 there were six reports relating to health covering topics as diverse as use of agency nurses, the national programme for IT, financial management in the NHS, out-of-hours care; the Paddington basin health campus and obesity (House of Commons Committee of Public Accounts 2007a–f).

The Department of Health is also required to present a departmental report to parliament each year that provides an account of how it has spent its allocated resources, as well as its future planned spending. It also describes policies and programmes, and gives a breakdown of spending within these programmes (Department of Health 2007c).

There have been various suggestions recently that parliament should regain more political weight in British politics to counter the 'presidential-style' decision-making (Richards and Smith 2002) characterised by the leadership style of Tony Blair, and Margaret Thatcher before him. The new Prime Minister, Gordon Brown, announced to the House of Commons on 3 July 2007 that he wishes to agree 'a new constitutional settlement that entrusts more power to Parliament and the British people' – a proposal that has been welcomed by the Public Administration Select Committee (2007b).

Arguably, parliament already plays an active role in holding ministers to account. According to Paton (2007, p 67):

> ... both under the Major governments from 1992 to 1997 and after 2005 in New Labour's third term with a reduced majority, backbenchers and indeed the House of Lords have inflicted significant pressure and actual defeats upon the government of the day.

Indeed, health legislation, to abolish community health councils, establish foundation trust hospitals and reform the Mental Capacity Bill, encountered a great deal of opposition from backbench MPs. Although the government got each of the Bills through parliament, scrutiny of this sort can result in amendments to legislation. The Health Committee has also been active and at times highly critical of Labour's post-2002 health reforms despite its majority of Labour MPs (Health Committee 2007).

We suggest that parliamentary accountability could be strengthened in a number of ways.

■ First, by providing greater resources to the Health Committee to carry out its existing remit of monitoring government or by expanding its powers so that it could perform a much more visible role in carrying out parliamentary scrutiny (as suggested below).

■ Second, by requiring reports to be laid before parliament for debate. At present the Healthcare Commission reports to parliament annually on the state of health care in England and Wales (Healthcare Commission 2006). Monitor is also required to lay before parliament an annual report and a summary of the accounts of NHS foundation trusts (NHS Act 2006, Schedule 8). The new health care and social care regulator proposed for 2008 will be responsible for quality and safety standards of all health care and social care providers (both public and private). To ensure that it is properly accountable for carrying out this task, it will be important that a report continues to be set before parliament. It could be subjected to parliamentary debate and scrutiny by the Health Committee, along with other key annual reports. At present the Chief Medical Officer's annual report is presented to government rather than to parliament. It provides an independent account on the state of public health, and could be presented alongside the regulator's report on the state of health care to parliament. The NHS Chief Executive's annual report, in contrast, has no independent status at present. In future this report could be submitted to parliament alongside the departmental report (prepared by the Permanent Secretary) for debate and scrutiny by parliament. These reports would in effect reflect the triumvirate structure created by the most recent reorganisation in the Department of Health (*see* p 23). If the Health Committee were to examine these reports (and their associated plans) more systematically, it would need an independent assessment (for example, by the National Audit Office (NAO)) to inform its work.

- Third, parliament could be given a greater role in pre- and post-legislative scrutiny of health reforms. The Public Administration Select Committee (2007a) report on the machinery of government requested that a more formal process of parliamentary scrutiny be introduced before major reforms to the machinery of government are undertaken. This process would require that both houses of parliament give their assent to significant changes, after being presented with a business case in which an accurate estimate of costs were made. The Public Administration Select Committee argues that this process would force politicians and policy-makers to explain the reasoning behind proposed changes and the evidence supporting them. Potentially major reforms and restructuring of the NHS could be subject to similar pre-legislative scrutiny. A more formal process of scrutiny could prevent ill-thought-through and poorly costed reform proposals from being introduced and provide 'a worthwhile check on unilateral action' (PASC 2007a, p 12). In particular, it would provide an extra layer of defence against the problem of 'continuous structural reforms'. One obvious danger of introducing pre-legislative scrutiny is that it might slow reforms to such an extent that it paralyses the NHS, so even where change is needed in response to a changing environment this is not possible.

- Another tool that could be used more effectively for pre-legislative scrutiny of policies is regulatory impact assessments (RIAs). These are tools for assessing 'the need for and impact of proposed regulation and amendments to existing regulations' (NAO 2007, p 4). Currently all policies are required to have a regulatory impact assessment. Unfortunately, these are often prepared at a late stage in the policy development process and therefore have little impact on the final content of policy before it is introduced. The NAO found that regulatory impact assessments were not normally used by parliament and select committees to inform parliamentary debates over proposed policies and legislation, although there is nothing to stop them doing so at present.

■ Finally, parliament could have a role in post-legislative scrutiny. The Law Commission (2006, p 7) defines post-legislative scrutiny as 'a broad form of review, the purpose of which is to address the effects of the legislation in terms of whether the intended policy objectives have been met by the legislation and, if so, how effectively'. Both the Law Commission (2006) and the Hansard Society (Brazier 2005) have recommended that parliament should systematically review the laws that it passes. Parliament would look at whether its intentions had been met and what, if any, unintended consequences had arisen. It could highlight any 'implementation gaps' and other obstacles to the successful delivery of policy aims. The Better Regulation Executive, as part of its principles of better regulation, suggests the possibility of including sunset clauses in legislation. This provides an opportunity for the legislation to be reviewed and amended before being readopted or extended (Better Regulation Task Force 2003).

By strengthening the role of parliament in scrutinising health and health care policies as part of wider constitutional reforms, it will be better equipped to carry out its role as a watchdog of government action. We suggest that, by strengthening parliamentary scrutiny of the activities of the Department of Health, the problems of excessive ministerial control and centralisation of health policy decisions would be reduced.

Redefine the 'bedpan' doctrine

Aneurin Bevan's 'bedpan' doctrine – that the noise of a dropped bed pan should resound in the Palace of Westminster – in practice means that the Secretary of State for Health is called to account when there are high-profile failures in local health services. Glasby *et al* (2006) cite the example of the inquiry that followed media coverage of dead bodies on the floor of a chapel in Bedford Hospital. In an organisation of the size and complexity of the NHS, it is not sensible for ministers to be held accountable every time something goes wrong locally, in particular for actions for which they are not responsible. The 'bedpan' doctrine inevitably results in ministers getting involved in the micromanagement of providers.

Failures in local service provision are increasingly matters for local boards. As the remaining NHS trusts are either authorised as foundation trusts or taken over by, closed or merged with foundation trusts, direct lines of accountability from government ministers to the providers of health care will be severed. Local management will be responsible for running services, and will be held to account locally by their boards, which will monitor their performance, and be subject to independent regulation to assure standards. It is not clear that all policy-makers, senior managers or foundation trust governors understand these new relationships and the significance of these changes. Certainly most professionals, patients and the public do not. It will be important to be clear where accountability rests for failures experienced by patients in the delivery of high-quality, safe and effective care.

The pressure to intervene might ease if ministers were consistent in refusing to be drawn into discussions about local service issues. This requires civil servants to advise ministers on how to avoid getting drawn in and for special advisers and communication teams to exercise restraint. The media too would need to alter the way in which they report on health stories so that chief executives and chairs of trusts are interviewed rather than ministers when there is a high-profile service failure. The media coverage after the recent Healthcare Commission report into the case of Maidstone and Tunbridge Wells NHS Trust, where 90 patients died after contracting *Clostridium difficile* (Healthcare Commission 2007b), shows how difficult it is for ministers not to be drawn in.

However, service failures are not always simply a result of local action (or lack of it), but may also be a consequence of national policy. If national policy is a contributing factor it is right that ministers be questioned on the issue and that the public holds them to account.

In addition, the incentives and pressures for the Secretary of State and ministers to get involved in local management issues need to be removed (Greer 2005). Governments are tempted to interfere when levers and incentives in the system appear not to be producing the desired results, so it is important to ensure that the incentives faced by other bodies and health care organisations are aligned with government objectives. Ministers are likely to get drawn in to some local issues via PCTs, particularly if improvements are not as rapid as they expect. In principle, however, issues of quality and safety failure should be a matter for the new health and social care regulator in future and financial failure for Monitor.

We suggest that the 'bedpan' doctrine is redefined so that the sound of a dropped bedpan echoes in the offices of local hospital management. Ministers must resist being drawn in to comment on every problem with local services. However, where such problems arise as a consequence of the shortcomings of national policies or highlight problems that may be more widespread, it may be appropriate for ministers to take responsibility for addressing these issues.

Strengthen local accountability

As the section on the history of the NHS (above) demonstrated, there has been a growing tendency for local NHS bodies to be tightly controlled by the Department of Health. This tendency is reinforced by the vertical lines of accountability that run from local health care organisations up to the Department of Health and the Secretary of State. Those who support an independent board to oversee PCTs believe that it will reduce central control of the NHS. We suggest that another option is to strengthen local accountability of PCTs.

Although PCTs are accountable to ministers via SHAs and the Department of Health for their overall performance, they are also subject to a raft of other forms of accountability. The Healthcare Commission collects information on their performance, for example, against a set of standards laid down by the Department of Health. The Healthcare Commission has also been asked to develop more comprehensive performance criteria for PCTs by the Department of Health. In future, PCTs will be assessed jointly with local authorities and other area-based stakeholders, which will be monitored as part of the comprehensive area assessment (Department for Communities and Local Government 2006). The Audit Commission has responsibility for holding them accountable for their financial management. As with NHS providers, PCTs are subject to local authority overview and scrutiny committees. There is currently significant confusion about the system of performance management and performance assessment for PCTs. Local accountability would need to be sufficiently robust to substitute for some of these mechanisms; if it were introduced in addition to existing lines of accountability, there is a danger PCTs would be pulled in different directions.

Local accountability of PCTs could take a number of forms.

- **Foundation PCTs** Give PCTs similar levels of autonomy to foundation trusts if they are able to demonstrate sound financial and corporate governance. Members of PCTs, drawn from the geographical catchment area of the PCT, would be eligible to vote. The board of governors of the PCT would hold the executive to account.

- **Local authority commissioning** Local authorities would be charged with commissioning health services (or contracting with a commissioning organisation to procure services) – akin to the model of health care in Denmark, Sweden and Norway where local elected officials in the county councils are responsible for health care.

- **Direct elections to PCTs** Board members of PCTs could be directly elected. The difference between this option and that described above is that the electorate would be all those eligible to vote in local elections (it assumes co-terminosity with local authorities).

- **Overview and scrutiny committees** Increase the power of overview and scrutiny committees beyond their right to refer decisions on reconfiguration of local services to the Secretary of State (Lewis *et al* 2006). In contrast to patient and public involvement (PPI) forums and Local Involvement Networks (LINkS) in future, overview and scrutiny committees do have powers to scrutinise local health care services but their powers to intervene are at present weak. Overview and scrutiny committees are made up of elected local councillors.

In assessing the merits of creating foundation PCTs, evidence on the governance of foundation trusts should be taken into account. Early evidence suggests that governors think that their role is ill defined and perceive that they have little impact on decisions, which suggests that further effort is required to improve the effectiveness of the new local governance arrangements (Lewis and Hinton 2008). Regulation appears at present to be a stronger form of accountability. Monitor is responsible for authorising foundation trusts and has an ongoing role in relation to their financial health and governance. The Healthcare Commission is responsible for monitoring and enforcing foundation trusts' quality and safety standards.

Although foundation status has been accepted and implemented for providers, there is ongoing debate with respect to PCTs. The latter are entrusted with taxpayers' money and are expected to purchase (and provide) health services on behalf of their local populations and improve health more generally. Given the amount of public money that they spend and the importance of commissioning decisions in determining how and where money is spent, it is likely that the public will expect them to be democratically accountable. Although the new regulator will assure the quality and safety of PCT provision if PCTs were to be given foundation status, there would need to be a body similar to Monitor that could assess and monitor their financial and quality performance as commissioners.

Alternative models, at present, seem less plausible (*see* Lewis *et al* 2008). Local authority commissioning would change the balance of power between local authorities and central government and might

require a major change in the way that health care is funded (Glasby
et al 2006). In countries where local government is responsible for
health care, funding is mainly through local taxation (with some
national subsidies, to reduce differences in levels of funding caused by
variations in average income by county). Otherwise, there would need
to be huge increases in the transfers from central government to local
government, fuelling further the debate about whether the NHS is a
national health service any longer. There is no tradition of direct election
to public office in England and experience in other countries is variable,
although such an approach has been successfully introduced in New
Zealand and Canada. The involvement of local authority overview and
scrutiny committees in relation to NHS reconfiguration debates has
not been without controversy. Recent Department of Health policy is
encouraging overview and scrutiny committees to focus particularly on
the work of commissioners of health care and social care (Department
of Health 2006c). Given plans to set shared targets under local
area agreements, there might be some merits in exploring the role
of overview and scrutiny committees further. Any changes to the
accountability of PCTs need to recognise the plethora of relationships
that they already have with other bodies.

Strengthening local accountability is one possible way in which
accountability of commissioners can be enhanced, although caution
should be exercised. Policy-makers should not rush to create
foundation PCTs without an independent examination of the ability
and legitimacy that governors have to hold foundation trust boards
to account and a better understanding of the regulatory framework
needed. Independent assessment of PCT performance against
defined objectives by the Healthcare Commission and as part of the
comprehensive area assessment at least mean that performance
assessment is becoming less politicised. It is likely that the government
will continue to require PCTs to be democratically accountable, and
therefore they are unlikely to relinquish control of commissioning to
a regulator.

Increase transparency

If health policy is to be seen as less politicised it needs to be more transparent about the evidence on which decisions are based.

The government recognised the need for better policy-making and was committed to promoting evidence-based policy-making as early as 1999 when it published the White Paper *Modernising Government* (Cabinet Office 1999). It was followed by a series of government documents that sought to strengthen departmental analytical and modelling capabilities (Cabinet Office 2000), pilot reforms and policies before rolling them out (Cabinet Office 2003), and to improve the quality of research commissioned by departments (Comptroller and Auditor General 2003a). The latest Capability Review of the Department of Health suggests that it still has some way to go in meeting the expectations for better policy-making set out in the 1999 White Paper *Modernising Government* (Cabinet Office 2007).

Ideally, data on the process of decision-making, the evidence for decisions and the data used should be made available. To maintain public trust in the health system, it is important that the Department of Health and ministers make publicly available information on policy decisions and the evidence underpinning them. This will reduce the perception of the general public and of NHS staff that policies are ill thought through and politically motivated.

The introduction of the Freedom of Information Act 2000 has meant that public bodies are more 'open' than in the past, although the government has sought to place limits on the number of requests and changed the fee schedule. Roberts (2006) identified a number of perverse responses to this Act by government and public bodies, such as changes in record keeping, veto of politically sensitive requests, under-resourcing of Freedom of Information offices and delays in releasing information. Certainly the Freedom of Information Act has affected what is recorded and how record keeping is organised within government departments. The possibility of requesting information makes policy-making more open, but this is not the same as an organisation operating in an open and transparent manner and proactively providing information. There is still room for improvement in the openness and transparency of health policy-making in England.

The Department of Health, and the other public bodies to which the Department of Health has delegated responsibility and decision-making, must operate in a transparent manner that promotes public confidence. Public bodies have different rules governing whether meetings are held in public, minutes and proceedings are published and what information must be contained in annual reports. The government should be clearer about the level of openness that it expects from health care organisations, whether they be regulators, commissioners or providers.

Create an NHS constitution

The government has recently announced that it is considering drawing up an NHS constitution (Department of Health 2007f). The decision as to whether there is a case for a constitution will be decided by the time of the final report of the national review led by Sir Ara Darzi.

The idea was first raised by Andy Burnham, the then Minister of Health, in a letter to the then Secretary of State for Health, Patricia Hewitt. He wrote:

> *An NHS Constitution could provide a clear expression of what is unchanging about the NHS and what we hold in common. It would set down and protect the values of what is a precious and unique British institution. It would provide a more secure framework within which debates about change can take place. In itself, it would be an important symbol that what is special about the NHS is not the buildings or services but its values and principles.*
> (Burnham 2007, p 6).

Burnham went on to write:

> *If handled correctly, a Constitution could seal a generational consensus around the NHS model that would help defuse the ideological and political wrangling that staff find destabilising. Like the BBC Charter, it could prompt a periodic public debate about what the NHS is and should seek to do, a process that would be healthy and renewing.*
> (Burnham 2007, p 7).

The BMA has also advocated for a constitution. The constitution would set out the core values, a charter of rights and responsibilities, and a definition of the services that are nationally available and quality standards for those services (BMA 2007).

It is not clear what form a constitution would take. Generally, a constitution denotes something that is relatively unchanging. As it sets out fundamental political or social rights and the process by which these are upheld, amendments usually require passage through a more exacting legislative process. One might therefore anticipate that an NHS constitution would be set out in a piece of primary legislation, possibly with additional caveats to prevent amendment without cross-party support. The exact legal form and the implications for the parliamentary process need to be more thoroughly worked through by constitutional lawyers. If it could be changed easily by each new government or administration, it would not reduce politicisation of the NHS.

As a result of devolution there is divergence in the health care policies being pursued in each part of the UK. Given that the British government has responsibility for the NHS only in England it is reasonable to assume that the proposed NHS constitution would apply only there. If different health care rights were conferred on residents in England, this might fuel political demands for greater equity as occurred after the introduction of personal care without charge for older people in

Scotland. If the NHS constitution did not confer any legally enforceable rights or guarantees it would, similar to the Patients' Charter before it, be seen as a political device that simply raises expectations, which then cannot be met. Indeed it would hardly be worthy of being called a constitution.

In the government's most recent proposals a number of suggestions have been put forward as to what might be included in a constitution: a statement of values, a framework for accountability, a list of responsibilities for all who work for NHS patients, the process of arbitration on local reconfiguration decisions, set of rights and responsibilities, rights of public involvement, opportunities for partnership working and the process for making NHS appointments (Department of Health 2007f). This is a wide-ranging list and suggests a lack of clarity among policy-makers at present as to the purpose of a constitution. We consider the value of an NHS constitution in relation to a number of these ideas.

Setting out the values of the NHS would not prove politically contentious – there appears to be little disagreement about the underlying values or principles of the NHS. In fact the Conservative Party proposes to include the core NHS principles that were first set out in the NHS Plan in legislation (Table 1, overleaf). These hardly differ from the principles set out in the NHS Act 1946 and subsequent Acts. The Department of Health has already consulted on a set of principles that it anticipated would be included in all contracts for NHS care from April 2007 (Department of Health 2006d). The model NHS contract for 2007/8 included the following clause: 'The Parties shall have regard to the published statement of NHS principles.' It is not clear what these principles mean in practice because they would be difficult to enforce contractually as no measures are specified against which compliance could be assessed. They are currently aspirational rather than enforceable.

TABLE 1: NHS PRINCIPLES: CONSERVATIVE PARTY PROPOSALS VERSUS NHS PLAN

Conservative Party (2007)	Department of Health (2006b, 2006d)
The NHS will provide a universal service for all based on clinical need, not ability to pay	The NHS will provide a universal and comprehensive service with equal access for all, free at the point of use, based on clinical need, not ability to pay
The NHS will provide a comprehensive range of services	We will help keep people healthy and work to reduce health inequalities
The NHS will shape its services around the needs and preferences of individual patients, their families and their carers	We will work continuously to improve quality and safety
The NHS will respond to different needs of different populations	We will strive for the most effective and sustainable use of resources
The NHS will work continuously to improve quality services and to minimise errors	We will treat every patient with dignity and respect
The NHS will support and value its staff	We will shape our services around the needs and preferences of individual patients, their families and their carers
Public funds for health care will be devoted solely to NHS patients	We are committed to equality and non-discrimination
The NHS will work together with others to ensure a seamless service for patients	We will support and value our staff
The NHS will help keep people healthy and work to reduce health inequalities	We will work in partnership with others to ensure a seamless service for patients
The NHS will respect the confidentiality of individual patients and provide open access to information about services, treatment and performance	We will respect the confidentiality of individual patients and provide open access to information about services, treatment and performance

How would a constitution clarify what the NHS is and how it operates? This is easier said than done. Most people still equate the NHS with its institutions. It was the hospitals that were nationalised at the creation of the NHS and have been the most visible and tangible part of the NHS through its 60-year history. One only has to follow the arguments about the privatisation of the NHS to see that the NHS is thought of as a collection of publicly owned and publicly run facilities (Pollock 2004). The pace of change means that there is currently a mismatch between the public and professional understanding of the NHS, as a public provider of health care, and its major role as a payer and commissioner of care. Setting out this version of the NHS explicitly could be politically challenging.

Recent government proposals suggest that a constitution might also set out the processes for decision-making on both controversial issues, such as reconfiguration, and less controversial ones, such as NHS appointments. It might also set out requirements for public involvement and accountability. There is currently a cacophony of accountability mechanisms facing providers and commissioners. These may duplicate in some areas but leave accountability gaps in others. It is also often not clear the extent to which different organisations have discretion or freedom to operate in particular ways, for example, in partnership with the private sector or local government. There is a need to clarify how different organisations in the new NHS, including regulators, relate to each other and to the Department of Health or parliament. However, no one could seriously suggest setting current organisational forms and institutional arrangements in a constitution – that would in effect place a preservation order on the status quo.

Finally, there is the suggestion that a constitution might set out rights and responsibilities. One option is to define a national benefits package, another is simply to set out the standards of care that patients can already expect as a set of guarantees or rights (for example, waiting times of 18 weeks from referral to treatment).

The idea of a benefits package and the difficulties of priority setting have been discussed elsewhere (Ham and Coulter 2000; Robinson and Dixon 2000). In Germany the Social Code Book V broadly sets out the entitlements that members of the statutory health insurance system can expect. The detailed decisions about which services are reimbursable and the value of the reimbursement are decided by the Federal Joint Committee on the basis of advice from the National Institute of Quality and Efficiency (Lewis *et al* 2006). Decisions on the eligibility of individual cases are made by the social courts. If a constitution that defined entitlements was to have legal standing, such as in Germany, it would require the government to make more explicit what the NHS does and does not cover, a process for drawing up a detailed catalogue of benefits and a means for appeals to be heard in individual cases.

High-profile media coverage of differential availability of new drug treatments suggest that the public do not find it acceptable to have geographical variations in treatments. Such cases have often precipitated political interference, for example, in the case of Herceptin. It has been suggested that NICE take a more comprehensive approach to coverage decisions, determining a package of services and treatments to be funded by the NHS (Robinson and Dixon 2000; Williams 2004). Decisions on the inclusion of new benefits would have to be linked to the size and growth of the NHS budget. Currently local PCT committees have to make decisions on exceptional cases where there is either no NICE guidance or a clinician believes that there are exceptional circumstances, which mean that a patient should have the treatment funded. If entitlements were legally enforceable, this process would probably be replaced by court decisions unless existing processes were placed on a statutory footing.

Even with a national benefits package, there would be variations based on clinical prioritisation and there may also be some legitimate reasons for variation. It is also not clear how such a move fits in with guidance to

PCTs that they should commission non-clinical services if these promote well-being and independence (Department of Health 2007b).

The alternative option would be simply to make explicit the minimum standards of care that patients can expect. These would be a means of translating the targets (now met) and policy commitments into a document directed at patients. This might include, for example, choice of any registered provider at point of referral and a maximum 18-week wait from referral to treatment. This would be similar to the Patients' Charter and may suffer from a lack of credibility with the public if these 'rights' were not enforceable.

So, at a minimum a constitution could restate the fundamental principles and values of the NHS. It could also set out how the new NHS is constituted following the implementation of system reforms, however, this might prove politically controversial. To address the fundamental concerns raised by the proponents of the independent board, that the NHS is politicised by ministerial interference and micromanaged by the Department of Health, an 'internal constitution' might be the answer. This was suggested 10 years ago but is still valid today:

> *For nearly 50 years, the NHS has struggled to find the right balance between centre and periphery. ... What is needed now is a renegotiation of the internal constitution in the light of a proper appreciation of the growing complexity of the NHS and the factors underlying it. Such a renegotiation might involve imposing restrictions on the role of the centre and the explicit creation of scope for local initiative.*
> (King's Fund Policy Institute 1997)

We suggest that while the idea of an NHS constitution has potential there needs to be more thought given to the objectives, the form that it will take and the process for agreeing and revising it in future. If a constitution were to establish fundamental rights and entitlements, this would require considerable technical work and extensive public debate and could open the way for litigation. If it does little more than restate the core principles of the NHS, it will not be worthy of being called an 'NHS constitution'. We suggest that it might set out the roles and relationships of key actors in the health system, including the Department of Health, and make clear how the NHS is governed.

Conclusions

It is perhaps ironic that, just as reforms are being implemented that are designed to devolve greater responsibility to local health care organisations, there are calls for the handing over of responsibilities from central government to an independent board. This paper has argued that this would be a step in the wrong direction. An independent board is a misguided solution to the problems of how to reduce excessive political interference, centralisation and micromanagement of the NHS.

These problems are not new. Since the establishment of the NHS there have been ongoing debates about the appropriate roles of central government and local providers, of politicians and managers. Attempts in the past to give central managerial control to a single body and to separate policy formulation and management did not succeed in either improving the efficiency of delivery or reducing political interference.

Instead we suggest a number of alternative ideas as to how legitimate concerns about excessive ministerial and central control could be addressed. We think policy-makers should give further consideration to the following suggestions: adopting the principle of subsidiarity, strengthening the role of parliament, redefining the bedpan doctrine, strengthening local accountability, increasing transparency and creating an NHS constitution. An NHS constitution that clarified the roles and relationships in the new health care system, in particular the lines of accountability and the responsibility for decision-making, would ensure that despite a more complex system, it would be clear how the NHS is governed and place appropriate legal checks on ministerial and departmental decisions.

References

Banks T (1994). *Review of the Wider Department of Health*. London: Department of Health.

Better Regulation Task Force (BRTF) (2003). *Principles of Good Regulation*. Available at: www.brc.gov.uk/upload/assets/www.brc.gov.uk/ principlesleaflet.pdf (accessed on 20 July 2007).

Bevan G (2006). 'A third way'. *British Medical Journal*, vol 333, p 252.

Bevan G, Hood C (2006). 'What's measured is what matters: targets and gaming in the English public health care system'. *Public Administration*, vol 84, no 3, pp 517–38.

Blair T (2007). Speech on the National Health Service at the King's Fund, London on 30 April 2007. Available at: www.number-10.gov.uk/output/Page11575.asp (accessed on 29 May 2007).

Brazier A (2005). *Post-legislative Scrutiny. Issues in Law Making 6*. London: Hansard Society.

British Medical Association (2007). *A Rational Way Forward for the NHS in England*. London: BMA. Available at: www.bma.org.uk/ap.nsf/ AttachmentsByTitle/PDFrationalwayforward/$FILE/rationalwayforward.pdf (accessed on 18 May 2007).

Brown G (2007). Speech to Labour Party Conference, 24 September 2007. Available at: www.labour.org.uk/conference/brown_speech (accessed on 05 October 2007).

Brown G (2006). *We will always strive to be on your side*. Speech at Labour Party Conference, Manchester on 25 September 2006. Available at: www.epolitix.com/EN/News/200609/8f798088-0278-4909-8484- 30d61536f02d.htm (accessed on 7 November 2007).

Buchan J, Evans D (2007). *Realising the Benefits? Assessing the implementation of Agenda for Change*. London: King's Fund. Available at: www.kingsfund.org.uk/publications/kings_fund_publications/realising_the.html (accessed on 1 November 2007).

Burnham A (2007). *Days Out in the NHS: Listening to NHS staff*. Available at: www.dh.gov.uk/en/Publicationsandstatistics/Publications/PublicationsPolicyAndGuidance/DH_064715 (accessed on 18 May 2007).

Burnham A (2006). 'An NHS constitution could help unite the coalition of support for the health service'. *Progress*[online]. Available at: http://progressonline.org.uk/Magazine/article.asp?a=1399 (accessed on 18 May 2007).

Cabinet Office (2007). *Capability Review of the Department of Health*. London: Cabinet Office. Available at: www.civilservice.gov.uk/documents/capability/pdf/Capability_Review_DfH.pdf (accessed on 7 November 2007).

Cabinet Office (2006). *Public Bodies 2006*. London: Cabinet Office. Available at: www.civilservice.gov.uk/other/agencies/publications/pdf/public-bodies/publicbodies2006.pdf (accessed on 25 June 2007).

Cabinet Office (2003). *Trying it out. The role of pilots in policy-making*. Available at: www.cabinetoffice.gov.uk/strategy/downloads/su/pilots/html/downloads/rop.pdf (accessed on 14 August 2007).

Cabinet Office (2000). *Adding it up. Improving analysis and modelling in central government*. Available at: www.cabinetoffice.gov.uk/strategy/downloads/su/adding/coiaddin.pdf (accessed on 14 August 2007).

Cabinet Office (1999). *Modernising Government*. CM 4310. London: The Stationery Office. Available at: www.policyhub.gov.uk/docs/modgov.pdf (accessed on 14 August 2007).

Cameron D (2006). Speech at the King's Fund, London, 9 October 2006. Available at: www.kingsfund.org.uk/resources/events/past_events/conservative.html (accessed on 29 May 2007).

Carvel J (2007). 'NHS prepares for independence under Brown'. *The Guardian*. Available at: www.guardian.co.uk/print/0,,329821829-103690,00.html (accessed on 18 May 2007).

Chief Medical Officer (2005). *Annual Report*. London: Department of Health.

Comptroller and Auditor General (2003). *Getting the Evidence: Using research in policy making*. London: The Stationery Office. Available at: www.nao.org.uk/pn/02-03/0203586.htm (accessed on 14 August 2007).

Conservative Party (2007). *NHS Autonomy and Accountability. Proposals for legislation*. Available at: www.conservatives.com/pdf/NHSautonomyandaccountability.pdf (accessed on 6 November 2007).

Conservative Party (2003). *Setting the NHS Free. A Conservative policy consultation*. Available at: www.conservatives.com/getfile.cfm?file=HealthConsultationPaper&ref=POLICYDOCUMENT/1664&type=pdf (accessed on 18 May 2007).

Day P, Klein R (2007). *The Politics of Scrutiny. Reconfiguration in NHS England*. London: Nuffield Trust. Available at: www.nuffieldtrust.org.uk/ecomm/files/Politics%20of%20Scrutiny.pdf (accessed on 10 July 2007).

Day P, Klein R (2000). 'The politics of managing the National Health Service' in Rhodes RAW (ed), *Transforming British Government. Vol 1: Changing Institutions*, pp 238–53. Basingstoke: Macmillan Press.

Day P, Klein R (1997). *Steering but not Rowing? The transformation of the Department of Health: a case study*. Bristol: The Policy Press.

Department for Communities and Local Government (2006). *Strong and Prosperous Communities. The Local Government White Paper*. CM 6939. Available at: http://www.communities.gov.uk/documents/localgovernment/pdf/154067 (accessed on 10 July 2007).

Department of Health (2007a). *Annual Reports*[online]. Available at: www.dh.gov.uk/en/Publicationsandstatistics/Publications/AnnualReports/index.htm (accessed on 20 July 2007).

Department of Health (2007b). *Choice Matters 2007–8. Putting patients in control*. London: Department of Health. Available at: www.dh.gov.uk/en/Publicationsandstatistics/Publications/PublicationsPolicyAndGuidance/DH_076331 (accessed on 13 July 2007).

Department of Health (2007c). *Commissioning Framework for Health and Well-being*. London: Department of Health. Available at: www.dh.gov.uk/en/Publicationsandstatistics/Publications/PublicationsPolicyAndGuidance/DH_072604 (accessed on 5 November 2007).

Department of Health (2007d). *Framework for Procuring External Support for Commissioners (FESC)*[online]. Available at: www.dh.gov.uk/en/Publicationsandstatistics/Publications/PublicationsPolicyAndGuidance/DH_065818 (accessed on 20 October 2007).

Department of Health (2007e). 'Health and Social Care Outcomes and Accountability Framework'. Department of Health website. Available at: www.dh.gov.uk/en/Consultations/Closedconsultations/DH_075267 (accessed on 14 August 2007).

Department of Health (2007f). *Our NHS, Our Future. NHS Next Stage Interim Report*. London: DH. Available at: www.dh.gov.uk/prod_consum_dh/idcplg?IdcService=GET_FILE&dID=150497&Rendition=Web (accessed on 1 November 2007).

Department of Health (2006a). *A Stronger Local Voice: A framework for creating a stronger local voice in the development of health and social care services*. London: Department of Health. Available at: www.dh.gov.uk/en/Publicationsandstatistics/Publications/PublicationsPolicyAndGuidance/DH_4137040 (accessed on 13 July 2007).

Department of Health (2006b) 'Consultation on Core Principles for Everyone providing Care to NHS Patients.' Department of Health website. Available at: www.dh.gov.uk/en/Consultations/Liveconsultations/DH_064732 (accessed on 5 October 2007).

Department of Health (2006c). *The Future Regulation of Health and Adult Social Care in England.* London: Department of Health. Available at: www.dh.gov.uk/ en/Consultations/Closedconsultations/DH_063286 (accessed on 29 May 2007).

Department of Health (2006d). *The NHS in England: the Operating Framework for 2007/08.* London: Department of Health. Available at: www.dh.gov.uk/en/ Publicationsandstatistics/Publications/PublicationsPolicyAndGuidance/ DH_063267 (accessed on 29 May 2007).

Department of Health (2005a). *A Short Guide to NHS Foundation Trusts.* London: Department of Health. Available at: www.dh.gov.uk/en/ Publicationsandstatistics/Publications/PublicationsPolicyAndGuidance/ DH_4126013 (accessed on 31 July 2007).

Department of Health (2005b). *Commissioning a Patient Led NHS*[online]. Available at: www.dh.gov.uk/en/Publicationsandstatistics/Publications/ PublicationsPolicyAndGuidance/DH_4116716 (accessed on 20 October 2007).

Department of Health (2005c). *Departmental Report 2005.* London: Department of Health. Available at: www.dh.gov.uk/en/Publicationsandstatistics/ Publications/AnnualReports/DH_4113725 (accessed on 14 August 2007).

Department of Health (2004a). *Choosing Health. Making Healthy Choices Easier.* London: Department of Health. Cm 6374. Available at: www.dh.gov.uk/ en/Publicationsandstatistics/Publications/PublicationsPolicyAndGuidance/ DH_4094550 (accessed on 1 November 2007).

Department of Health (2004b). *Departmental Report 2004.* London: Department of Health. Available at: www.dh.gov.uk/en/Publicationsandstatistics/ Publications/AnnualReports/DH_4080936 (accessed on 14 August 2007).

Department of Health (2004c). *Reconfiguring the Department of Health's Arm's Length Bodies.* London: Department of Health. Available at: www.dh.gov.uk/ en/Publicationsandstatistics/Publications/PublicationsPolicyAndGuidance/ DH_4086081 (accessed on 13 July 2007).

Department of Health (2003). *Overview and Scrutiny of Health – Guidance.* London: Department of Health. Available at: www.dh.gov.uk/en/ Publicationsandstatistics/Publications/PublicationsLegislation/DH_4009607 (accessed on 13 July 2007).

Department of Health (2000). *The NHS Plan. A plan for investment. A plan for reform.* Cm 4818-I. London: The Stationery Office. Available at: www.dh.gov.uk/en/Publicationsandstatistics/Publications/ PublicationsPolicyAndGuidance/DH_4002960 (accessed on 10 July 2007).

Department of Health (1993). *Managing the New NHS.* London: Department of Health.

Dewar S (2003). *Government and the NHS: Time for a new relationship.* London: King's Fund. Available at: www.kingsfund.org.uk/resources/publications/ government_and.html (accessed on 10 July 2007).

Edwards B (2007a). *An Independent NHS: A review of the options.* London: The Nuffield Trust. Available at: http://nuffieldtrust.nvisage.uk.com/ecomm/files/ IndependentNHS.pdf (accessed on 10 July 2007).

Edwards N (2007b). *Lost in Translation: why are patients more satisfied with the NHS than the public?* London: NHS Confederation. Available at: www.nhsconfed.org/issues/issues-1739.cfm (accessed on 30 July 2007).

European Community (2002). *Consolidated Version of the Treaty Establishing the European Community.* Official Journal C 325. Available at http://eur-lex.europa.eu/en/treaties/dat/12002E/htm/12002E.html (accessed on 23 November 2007).

European Observatory on Healthcare Systems (1999). *Healthcare Systems in Transition. United Kingdom.* Available at: www.euro.who.int/document/ e68283.pdf (accessed on 20 June 2007).

Farrington-Douglas J, Brooks R (2007). *The Future Hospital: The politics of change.* London: Institute for Public Policy Research. Available at: www.ippr.org.uk/publicationsandreports/publication.asp?id=544 (accessed on 10 July 2007).

Glasby J, Smith J, Dickinson H (2006). *Creating NHS Local: A new relationship between PCTs and local government*. Birmingham: Health Services Management Centre School of Public Policy, University of Birmingham.

Godlee F (2006). 'Editor's choice'. *British Medical Journal*, vol 332. Available at: www.bmj.com/cgi/content/full/332/7544/0-f.

Greer S (2005). 'Why do good politics make bad health policy?' in Dawson S, Sausman C (eds), *Future Health Organisations and System*, pp 105–27. Basingstoke, Hampshire: Palgrave Macmillan.

Greer S, Jarman H (2007). *The Department of Health and the Civil Service. From Whitehall to department of delivery to where?* London: The Nuffield Trust. Available at: www.nuffieldtrust.org.uk/ecomm/files/DHCSW%20(final).pdf (accessed on 16 July 2007).

Griffiths R (1983). *NHS Management Inquiry: Report*. London: DHSS.

Ham C (2004). *Health Policy in Britain*. Basingstoke, Hampshire: Palgrave Macmillan.

Ham C, A Coulter (2000). *The Global Challenge of Health Care Rationing*. Philadelphia: Open University Press.

Hansard (2006). *NHS: Advisory Committee on Resource Allocation*. House of Lords, 1 February 2006 WA55. Available at: www.publications.parliament.uk/pa/ld200506/ldhansrd/vo060201/text/60201w02.htm (accessed on 10 July 2007).

Health Committee (2007). *Work of the Committee 2005–06*. 2nd Report of the Session 2006–7. HC 297. London: The Stationery Office. Available at: www.publications.parliament.uk/pa/cm200607/cmselect/cmhealth/297/297.pdf (accessed on 16 July 2007).

Healthcare Commission (2007a). *Independent Sector Treatment Centres. A review of the quality of care*. Available at: www.healthcarecommission.org.uk/_db/_documents/ISTC_Final_Tagged.pdf (accessed on 14 August 2007).

Healthcare Commission (2007b). *Investigation into outbreaks of* Clostridium difficile *at Maidstone and Tunbridge Wells NHS Trust*. Available at: www.healthcarecommission.org.uk/_db/_documents/ Maidstone_and_Tunbridge_Wells_investigation_report_Oct_2007.pdf (accessed on 20 October 2007).

Healthcare Commission (2006). *State of Healthcare 2006*. London: Commission for Healthcare Audit and Inspection. Available at: www.healthcarecommission.org.uk/_db/_documents/ State_of_Healthcare_2006_English_tagged_200701023846.pdf (accessed on 6 November 2007).

Healthcare for London (2006). *A Framework for Action*. London: Healthcare for London. Available at: www.healthcareforlondon.nhs.uk/ framework_for_action.asp (accessed on 15 August 2007).

Hewitt P (2007). Speech at the London School of Economics, London on 14 June 2007. Available at: www.lse.ac.uk/collections/pressAndInformationOffice/ newsAndEvents/archives/2007/PatriciaHewitt.htm (accessed on 10 July 2007).

Hoque K, Davis S, Humphreys M (2004). 'Freedom to do what you are told: Senior management team autonomy in an NHS acute trust'. *Public Administration*, vol 82, no 2, pp 355–75.

House of Commons Committee of Public Accounts (2007a). *Department of Health: Improving the use of temporary nursing staff in NHS acute and foundation trusts. Twenty-ninth Report of Session 2006–07*. HC 142. London: The Stationery Office. Available at: www.publications.parliament.uk/pa/ cm200607/cmselect/cmpubacc/142/142.pdf (accessed on 6 November 2007).

House of Commons Committee of Public Accounts (2007b). *Department of Health: The National Programme for IT in the NHS. Twentieth Report of Session 2006–07*, HC 390. London: The Stationery Office. Available at: www.publications.parliament.uk/pa/cm200607/cmselect/cmpubacc/390/ 390.pdf (accessed on 13 July 2007).

House of Commons Committee of Public Accounts (2007c). *Financial Management in the NHS. Seventeenth Report of Session 2006–07*, HC 361. London: The Stationery Office. Available at: www.publications.parliament.uk/ pa/cm200607/cmselect/cmpubacc/361/361.pdf (accessed on 13 July 2007).

House of Commons Committee of Public Accounts (2007d). *Tackling Child Obesity – First steps. Eighth Report of Session 2006–07*, HC 157. London: The Stationery Office. Available at: www.publications.parliament.uk/pa/cm200607/ cmselect/cmpubacc/157/157.pdf (accessed on 13 July 2007).

House of Commons Committee of Public Accounts (2007e). *The Paddington Health Campus Scheme. Ninth Report of Session 2006–07*, HC 244. London: The Stationery Office. Available at: www.publications.parliament.uk/pa/ cm200607/cmselect/cmpubacc/244/244.pdf (accessed on 13 July 2007).

House of Commons Committee of Public Accounts (2007f). *The Provision of Out-of-Hours Care in England*. Sixteenth Report of Session 2006-07, HC 360. London: The Stationery Office. Available at: www.publications.parliament.uk/ pa/cm200607/cmselect/cmpubacc/360/360.pdf (accessed on 13 July 2007).

Houses of Parliament (1973). *NHS Reorganisation Act 1973*. London: HMSO.

Hutton W (2000). *New Life for Health: The commission on the NHS*. London: Vintage.

Johnson A (2007) Speech to Labour Party Conference, 25 September 2007. Available at: www.labour.org.uk/conference/johnson_speech (accessed on 5 October 2007).

Klein R (2006). *The New Politics of the NHS. From Creation to Reinvention*, 5th ed. Oxford: Radcliffe Publishing.

King's Fund (2006). *Local Variations in NHS Spending Priorities*. London: King's Fund. Available at: www.kingsfund.org.uk/publications/briefings/ local_variations.html (accessed on 10 July 2007).

King's Fund (2005). *Policy Position: NICE and Herceptin*. London: King's Fund. Available at: www.kingsfund.org.uk/publications/briefings/ policy_position.html (accessed on 28 November 2007).

King's Fund (2002). *The Future of the NHS: A framework for debate*. London: King's Fund. Available at: www.kingsfund.org.uk/publications/ kings_fund_publications/the_future_of.html (accessed on 13 July 2007).

King's Fund Policy Institute (1997). 'A new constitution for the NHS' in Harrison T (ed), *Health Care UK 1996/97*. London: King's Fund.

Lamb N (2007). *Localism, Fairness and Empowerment in the NHS*. London: Liberal Democrats.

Law Commission (2006). *Post Legislative Scrutiny (Law Com No 302)*[online]. Available at: www.lawcom.gov.uk/docs/lc302.pdf (accessed on 13 July 2007).

Lewis R, Alvarez-Rosete A, Mays N (2006). *How to Regulate Healthcare in England? An international perspective*. London: King's Fund. Available at: www.kingsfund.org.uk/resources/publications/how_to_regulate.html (accessed on 18 May 2007).

Lewis R, Hinton L (2008). 'Citizen and staff involvement in health service decision-making: have National Health Service foundation trusts in England given stakeholders a louder voice?' *Journal of Health Services Research and Policy*, in press.

Lewis R, Thorlby R, Dixon J (2008). *Increasing the Public Accountability of Primary Care Trusts*. London: King's Fund, in press.

Monitor (2007). *NHS Foundation Trusts*. Available at: www.monitor-nhsft.gov.uk/ register_nhsft.php (accessed on 20 October 2007).

MORI (2007). *Political Monitor: Long Term Trends. The most important issues facing Britain today*. Available at: www.ipsos-mori.com/polls/trends/ issues_files/image002.gif (accessed on 5 October 2007).

Nairne P (1984). 'Parliamentary control and accountability' in Maxwell R, Weaver N (eds), *Public Participation in Health*, pp 33–51. London: King's Fund.

National Audit Office (2007). *Evaluation of Regulatory Impact Assessments 2006–07*. HC606. London: NAO. Available at: www.nao.org.uk/publications/nao_reports/06-07/0607606es.htm (accessed on 14 August 2006).

National Institute for Health and Clinical Excellence (2005). *A Guide to NICE*. London: NICE. Available at: www.nice.org.uk/page.aspx?o=guidetonice (accessed on 12 July 2007).

NHS Alliance (2000). *Implementing the Vision: Maintaining the values*. London: NHS Alliance.

NHS Confederation (2007). *From the Ground Up. How autonomy could deliver a better NHS*. Available at: www.nhsconfed.org/about/publications.cfm (accessed on 12 July 2007).

NHS Employers (2007). *NHS Employers – Pay and negotiations*. Available at: www.nhsemployers.org/pay-conditions/index.cfm (accessed on 10 August 2007).

Nugent N (1999). *The Government and Politics of the European Union*. Basingstoke: The Macmillan Press.

Paton C (2007). *New Labour's State of Health. Political economy, public policy and the NHS*. Aldershot, Hampshire: Ashgate.

Pollock A (2004). *NHS plc. The privatisation of our health care*. London: Verso.

Propper C, Sutton M, Whitnall C, Windmeijer F (2007). *Did 'Targets and Terror' Reduce English Waiting Times for Elective Hospital Care?* CMPO Working Paper 07/179. Bristol: University of Bristol.

Public Administration Select Committee (PASC) (2007a). *Machinery of Government Changes. Seventh Report of Session 2006–07*, HC 672. London: The Stationery Office. Available at: www.publications.parliament.uk/pa/cm200607/cmselect/cmpubadm/672/672.pdf (accessed on 16 July 2007).

Public Administration Select Committee (2007b). *The Governance of Britain. First Special Report of Session 2006–07*, HC 901. London: The Stationery Office. Available at: www.publications.parliament.uk/pa/cm200607/cmselect/cmpubadm/901/901.pdf (accessed on 16 July 2007).

Public Administration Select Committee (2003). *On Target? Government my measurement, vol. I. Fifth Report of Session 2002–03*, HC62-1. London: The Stationery Office. Available at: www.publications.parliament.uk/pa/cm200203/cmselect/cmpubadm/62/6202.htm (accessed on 29 May 2007).

Rayner B (1994). *History of the Department of Health*. London: Department of Health.

Revill J (2007). 'Brown rules out independence for the NHS'. *The Observer*. Available at: http://observer.guardian.co.uk/politics/story/0,,2073760,00.html (accessed on 17 May 2007).

Richards D, Smith MJ (2002). *Governance and Public Policy in the UK*. Oxford: Oxford University Press.

Roberts A (2006). 'Dashed expectations: governmental adaptation to transparency rules' in Hood C, Heald D (eds), *Transparency. The key to better governance?* pp 107–25. Oxford: The British Academy and Oxford University Press.

Robinson R, Dixon A (2000). *Completing the Course. Health to 2010*. London: Fabian Society.

Royal Commission on the National Health Service (1979). *Report*. Cmnd 7615. London: HMSO.

Sutton M, Gravelle H, Morris S, Leyland A, Windmeijer F, Dibben C, Muirhead M (2002). *Allocation of Resources to English Areas: Individual and small area determinants of morbidity and use of healthcare resources*. Report to the Department of Health. Edinburgh: Information and Statistics Division.

Thorlby R, Maybin J (2007). *NHS Finances 2006/7: From deficit to a sustainable surplus?* London: King's Fund. Available at: www.kingsfund.org.uk/publications/ briefings/nhs_finances.html (accessed on 5 October 2007).

Thorlby R, Dixon J, Dickson N (2007). 'Health for London: Showing England the Way?' *British Medical Journal*, vol 335, pp 108–9.

Timmins N (1995). *The Five Giants. A biography of the Welfare State.* London: Harper Collins.

Triggle N (2006). 'Does the NHS need to be set free?' *BBC News*, 18 December. Available at: http://news.bbc.co.uk/1/hi/health/6134028.stm (accessed on 17 May 2007).

United Kingdom Parliament (2007a). 'Committee of Public Accounts'. UK Parliament website. Available at: www.parliament.uk/ parliamentary_committees/committee_of_public_accounts.cfm

United Kingdom Parliament (2007b). 'Health Committee Remit'. UK Parliament website. Available at: www.parliament.uk/parliamentary_committees/ health_committee/health_committee_remit.cfm (accessed on 20 July 2007).

Walsh N, Maybin J, Lewis R (2007). 'So where are the alternative providers in primary care?' *British Journal of Healthcare Management*, vol 13, no 2, pp 43–6.

Wanless D, Appleby J, Harrison A, Patel D (2007). *Our Future Health Secured? A review of NHS funding and performance.* London: King's Fund.

Williams A (2004). *What could be Nicer than NICE?* London: Office for Health Economics.

Williams S, Buchan J (2006). *Assessing the new NHS Consultant Contract. A something for something deal?* London: King's Fund. Available at: www.kingsfund.org.uk/publications/kings_fund_publications/ assessing_the.html (accessed on 1 November 2007).

Linked publications

We publish a wide range of resources on health and social care.
See below for a selection. For our full range of titles, visit our website
at **www.kingsfund.org.uk/publications** or call Sales and Information
on 020 7307 2591.

Windmill 2007: The future of health care reforms in England
Sarah Harvey, Alasdair Liddell, Laurie McMahon

The NHS has undergone many reforms over the past decade. To test out where
the reforms – and interactions between them – might lead the NHS, the
King's Fund formed a partnership with Loop2, Monitor and Nuffield Hospitals
to produce Windmill 2007. This initiative included a two-day simulation of
a fictional but realistic health economy from 2008 to 2011 and extensive
discussions of the emerging findings from that event with clinicians, managers,
policy-makers, regulators and analysts. The paper discusses what lessons
can be learnt from the simulation and what messages there are for the health
system of the future.

June 2007 ISBN 978 1 85717 558 5 80 pages £8.50

How to Regulate Health Care in England? An international perspective
Richard Lewis, Arturo Alvarez-Rosete, Nicholas Mays

Across the world, the appropriate role of government in the planning and
delivery of public services has been the subject of intense debate: how should
the state control the provision of public services and how far should markets
be allowed to determine the provision of those services? One answer to
these questions is 'regulation' – ie, the creation of mechanisms that allow
governments to influence the behaviour of autonomous service providers.
This report compares the regulatory framework in four health systems: the

Autonomous Community of Catalonia in Spain, Germany, the Netherlands and New Zealand. This comparison is used to reflect on the future regulation of the NHS in England.

November 2006 ISBN 978 1 85717 554 7 84 pages £10.00

NHS Reform : Getting back on track
Keith Palmer

In recent years, the NHS has seen the most sustained period of funding growth ever. But despite the increased funding, the NHS is in deficit. In 2005/6, NHS trusts overspent by more than £1.2 billion and the NHS as a whole overspent by more than £500 million. This discussion paper looks at the causes of the NHS deficit in 2005/6. It then considers three recent policy developments – the 2006/7 system rules, the new payment by results tariffs and the commissioning framework – and asks what the impact of these policy developments could be and how they might be improved.

October 2006 ISBN 978 1 85717 552 3 78 pages £10.00

Designing the 'new' NHS: Ideas to make a supplier market in health care work
Nicholas Timmins (ed)

Recent changes in the NHS have triggered significant expansion in the involvement of independent and voluntary sectors in the delivery of services. How can this involvement be developed to ensure quality of care for patients and to enrich choice? This question was addressed by a small independent working group, commissioned by the King's Fund. This report is based on discussions within the group and on a one-day workshop that proposed and assessed alternative developments in the future NHS. This report highlights many of the issues that need to be addressed by government and by people providing health services in all three sectors.

June 2006 ISBN 978 1 85717 548 6 80 pages £5.00

How Should we Deal with Hospital Failure? Facing the challenges of the new NHS market
Keith Palmer

One in four NHS trusts in England ended 2004 in deficit. The impact of current NHS reforms will be to magnify financial imbalances at a significant number of trusts, with the risk that some of them will fail. But there is no real plan for dealing with failure in the NHS. This paper outlines proposals for dealing with financial instability by heading off failure before it happens and introducing a regime to manage those failures that cannot be averted. It emphasises the need for mechanisms that not only restore financial viability, but also protect the quality of patient care.

December 2005 ISBN 978 1 85717 542 4 60 pages £5.00

Regulating Health Care : The way forward
Jennifer Dixon

Reforms of the NHS are changing the role of the state in the provision of health care. Competition within the NHS (and with private providers) and the introduction of foundation trusts change the way in which providers should be regulated. This paper explores the impact of market incentives in the NHS on the regulatory regime and emphasises the importance of clarifying the respective roles of government and independent regulators. It suggests that economic regulation needs to be developed and aligned more closely with that in the private sector, and urges change to quality regulation, particularly in relation to improvement of performance.

December 2005 ISBN 978 1 85717 540 0 60 pages £5.00

The Future of Primary Care : Meeting the challenges of the new NHS market
Richard Lewis, Jennifer Dixon

Primary care has been the subject of a quiet revolution in recent years, with the ending of the monopoly of provision by independently contracted GPs and the introduction of a range of new targets and new forms of first contact care. Now it is poised for further radical change with reforms to the structure and roles of primary care trusts and the introduction of practice-based commissioning and competition between primary care providers. This paper examines the potential impact of these changes and the role of primary care in the new NHS market, outlining some of the main challenges and suggesting possible ways forward.

November 2005 ISBN 978 1 85717 536 3 32 pages £5.00

NHS Market Futures : Exploring the impact of health service market reforms
Richard Lewis, Jennifer Dixon

Despite initially rejecting the notion of an internal NHS market when it came to power in 1997, the Labour government has re-introduced competition to health services over the past three years. The market now emerging is the product of a series of separate policy developments – including extending choice of provider, expanding the role of the private sector and introducing payment by results – and consequently no one is sure what it will ultimately achieve. This paper analyses the government's market reforms, considering whether they can meet the core aims of the NHS, looking at the challenges they present, and exploring options for meeting those challenges.

September 2005 ISBN 978 1 85717 534 9 20 pages £5.00